Phil 1:6

Beyond the Cross

A Narrative of the Crucifixion, Resurrection, and Ascension of Christ

DR. HARRY E. CARR
TH.D., PH.D.

First Printing, April 2002

For additional copies, call or write to:

Shalom Baptist Church
3400 Morgan Road
Orion, MI 48359

(248) 391-0443
Fax: (248) 391-2928

ISBN: 0-9714699-2-X

Library of Congress Control Number:
2002092197

Printed in the United States by:
Morris Publishing
3212 East Highway 30
Kearney, NE 68847
1-800-650-7888

Dedication

Dedicated to my good friend…

Dr. Thomas Malone Sr.

Founder of
Emmanuel Baptist Church and
Midwestern Baptist College and
Seminary

With sincere thanks for his and
Mrs. Malone's encouragement in
my writing ministry.

Special Thanks

To my Shalom Baptist Church family for their faithful support of my ministry for over twenty-five years.

To Judy Heatherly, my church secretary of many years, whose devoted help in the church ministries provided some additional time for me to work on each manuscript.

To my wife, Alberta, and my family – Ann and Warren, David and Lisa, Lisa, and Gary, who all share my love for the Lord.

To all my grandchildren who keep "Papa" young, Jon, Micha'l, Candace, Kaitlyn, Courtney, Cayla, David Jr. and Shauni.

A very special thanks to Crystal Goldsworthy, my friend and secretary, who often devotes her own personal time to proof-read and format the manuscript, and for her encouragement to complete each manuscript.

* Cover picture courtesy of Dr. David M. Carr

Prologue

The events of our story will mostly stretch from late autumn of AD 29 until early summer of AD 30. That is with the exception of Jesus' appearance to Paul, which will not occur until some seven year later.

Since it is a narrative, certain parts of the story will be added. They will not be something way off base, but what common sense will supply in each situation. I have taken some liberties, not too many I hope, but I have tried to keep the story interesting and flowing. I have looked at seven different harmonies of the Gospel, all vary a little and in some places greatly. I have not followed any of them exactly, but have tried to give the date and place that seems appropriate to me.

This narrative is based on an early crucifixion. I do not know of any harmonies of the Gospel that agree with me, but then that does not change the Scriptures. It is absolutely impossible to get even three portions of a day from Friday until Sunday using the Jewish day. I believe that Jesus was crucified on Wednesday and arose sometime after sundown on Saturday, which is the Jewish day Sunday and is our Sunday after midnight. Don't give up on me too quickly. Hear me out and if we still disagree on the day of His crucifixion then we still agree that He was crucified.

I have tried to show you where Jesus was on certain dates and His activities. Follow on, as we trace those final days and the events that led to the cross and the resurrection beyond.

* All Scripture is quoted from the King James Version of the Bible.

Dr. Harry E. Carr
Orion, Michigan

Hebrew Calendar

Sacred Year Month	Civil Year Month	Hebrew Name	Modern Equivalent
1	7	Abib, or Nisan	April
2	8	Iyar, or Zif	May
3	9	Sivan	June
4	10	Tammuz	July
5	11	Ab	August
6	12	Elul	September
	New Year Begins		
7	1	Ethanim, or Tishri	October
8	2	Marcheshvan, or Bul	November
9	3	Chisleu	December
10	4	Tebeth	January
11	5	Shebat	February
12	6	Adar	March

* (Second Adar) ** This intercalary month was added about every three years

Note: The Jewish day began at 6:00 p.m. and ran through 6:00 p.m. the next day; therefore, the evening was the beginning of a new day.

Table of Contents

Part One – The Road to the Cross

Part Two – The Resurrection

Part One

The Road to the Cross

From Heaven He Came

From heaven He came,
    In the fullness of time.
Borne in His body,
    The sins that were mine.

Born of a virgin,
    In a manger He slept.
Bearing my sin,
    In a garden He wept.

Love so wondrous,
    Grace that was so kind.
Mercy bearing a cross,
    That should have been mine.

Wonderful Savior,
    Glorious friend.
How could my praises
    Ever find end?

Dr. Harry E. Carr
December 24, 1978

The Road to the Cross

Chapter One

The Beginning of the Last Days

Place: Jerusalem - At the Temple Date: 25 Chisleu AD 29

Jesus was in Jerusalem at the temple during the great Festival of Light (Hanukkah) on the twenty-fifth of the month of Chisleu (December) AD 29. There were now only four months left in the earthly ministry of Jesus. He was well aware that a run-in with the temple authorities and the Pharisees was inevitable. These last four months and the two months preceding them would be the months of the most serious confrontations with the Jerusalem religious authorities, and would begin the final phase of the road to the cross.

The confrontation would result in the religious authorities openly planning Jesus' death and being willing to pay someone among His followers to betray Him. Each step during those months led Jesus closer and closer to the final confrontation with the high priests and their sympathizers among the Sanhedrin Court.

At the Feast of Tabernacles

Place: Jerusalem - The Feast of Tabernacles   Date: Tisri AD 29

Jesus had spent the night in the Garden of Gethesame at the foot of the Mount of Olives. Early this morning, He came into one of the great porches of the temple. Soon a crowd had gathered around Him and He sat down and taught them.

The Pharisees and the Scribes had come upon an incident that they believed they could use against Jesus. It was concerning a woman who had been taken in the act of adultery, either by them or by someone who brought her to them.

They came half-dragging the young woman into the porch of the temple where Jesus sat teaching. All the attention of the crowd was fastened upon the scene. "This woman," they said, "was taken in the very act of adultery." It does make one wonder where the guilty man was, doesn't it? The very fact that the man was not brought with the woman shows that they had no desire for justice or for that matter the Law of Moses. It was clear and simple, they were setting a trap but you cannot fool an omniscient[1] Jesus. He saw not only though their intentions, but knew their sinful lives as well.

---

[1] Omniscient means *all knowing*. It is an attribute of God. Jesus possessed all the attributes of God; however, to make Himself like us, He voluntary limited them on occasion. At all times, He knew who He was and knew the thoughts and intentions of men.

The Scribes and Pharisees thought they had Jesus this time, for the woman had been taken in the act of adultery and the law of Moses, which they quickly quoted, called for her to be stoned. What hypocrites these men were. If the woman was caught, so was the man. Where was he? The penalty would have been the same for both, if it were ever carried out. In latter years, they had become quite lax in enforcing the law, choosing rather to put them out of the synagogue and refusing fellowship with the offenders.

"What shall we do with her," they asked? Now if they knew the answer, why did they ask Jesus? The Scribes were the experts in the law. Their very business was copying the Scriptures laboriously, word for word, page by page, until much of it was committed to memory.

They were often consulted by Pharisees and priests alike; however, the Sadducees seldom contacted them, except as a public display showing their support of them, for they did not believe in the inspired, infallible Word of God and consulted it only in cases of extreme emergency.

This situation had a double-barreled whammy. If Jesus said they should execute the woman by stoning, they could take it up with the Roman authorities, discrediting Jesus as a troublemaker. If He told them to release the woman, they would contend that He had no respect for the Law of Moses; therefore, discrediting Him before the very crowd He was teaching. They would contend that if He really was the Messiah, He would have great respect for the law of

God and would demand its fulfillment. Whatever decision Jesus made, they felt that they had Him this time.

Writing on the Ground

They had certainly underestimated Jesus. Stooping down, He wrote something on the ground, as if He did not hear them. The Bible does not say what Jesus wrote, but it must have been something that spoke to their hearts. Rising, He said...

> "He that is without sin among you, let him first cast a stone at her." John 8:7b

> "And again he stooped down, and wrote on the ground. And they which heard it, being convicted by their own conscience, went out one by one, beginning at the eldest, even unto the last: and Jesus was left alone, and the woman standing in the midst." John 8:8-9

As Jesus stooped to again write on the ground, a silence followed, and in the silence, their hearts stood still. What did Jesus know about them? Old sins, long hid in the secret closets of their hearts, came rushing back. The law condemned the wicked imagination of their hearts even if there were no actual incidents. Being convicted by their own enlightened consciences that were called to action by the words of Jesus, they begin to melt into the crowd and were soon gone. Isn't it strange that the older men were the first to go, followed by those that they had tried to lead into this travesty?

Jesus and the woman were left alone in the center of the crowd. She was alone, embarrassed, ashamed, and repentant. It must have been sincere; Jesus would have known.

> "When Jesus had lifted up himself, and saw none but the woman, he said unto her, Woman, where are those thine accusers? hath no man condemned thee? She said, No man, Lord. And Jesus said unto her, Neither do I condemn thee: go, and sin no more." John 8:10-11

Jesus' forgiveness also brought a sincere warning - stop practicing that sinful lifestyle. It isn't possible for man never to sin, but it is possible to let God clean up our life.

Jesus had fulfilled the Mosaical law. Why? Because the first accuser must cast the first stone against the accused, and he had disappeared into the crowd with the rest of them. The best-laid plans of men will always fail when they are directed against God.

Remember the beautiful words of Romans...

> "There is therefore now no condemnation to them which are in Christ Jesus, who walk not after the flesh, but after the Spirit." Romans 8:1

Enraging the Pharisees

The public defeat had not only embarrassed the authorities, it had enraged them. They were more determined than ever to expose

Jesus as a pseudo-Messiah.[2] Even though they were enraged, they were in the temple near the Treasury, and it was not a place where they would attack Jesus physically. It would be, with them, a war of words, name calling, and accusations. They attacked the virgin birth of Christ. Of course, they did not acknowledge this great doctrine but accused Jesus as one born of fornication, an illegitimate son. They played it up big that they were descendants of Abraham, and asked Jesus, "Who do you claim to be?"

The Eternal Jesus

Jesus made a strong public statement that incited the Pharisees to more than name-calling; it brought them to the point of inciting a riot.

> "Your father Abraham rejoiced to see my day: and he saw it, and was glad. Then said the Jews unto him, Thou art not yet fifty years old, and hast thou seen Abraham? Jesus said unto them, Verily, verily, I say unto you, Before Abraham was, I am." John 8:56-58

This was just too much. Before Abraham indeed! He wasn't even fifty years old and He claimed to precede Abraham. Those were the words of a demented man to them. What if He had told them about having lunch with Abraham in a tent near Hebron, and about taking a pleasant walk with him after lunch? The real explosion came when Jesus said, "Before Abraham was I am."

---

[2] Pseudo means *false, a counterfeit, an imposter*.

The words *"I am"* as it is used here, means I have always been, there was no time when I was not. The Pharisees recognized it as the title of deity. When Jesus identified Himself to Moses at the burning bush over 1500 years ago, He said, "I am that I am." [3] I am, I have always been and I will always be, that defines the eternity of God. Moses wrote the following in Psalm ninety...

> "Before the mountains were brought forth, or ever thou hadst formed the earth and the world, even from everlasting to everlasting, thou art God." Psalm 90:2

This was a clear claim that Jesus claimed to be God. It was so plain to the Pharisees; they took up stones to stone Jesus. Stoning was the penalty for blasphemy, and they considered Jesus to have just committed it openly and publicly. Rage gave way quickly to violence. The disciples would remember this occasion for the next six months. They must have thought, "we all shall surely die."

> "Then took they up stones to cast at him: but Jesus hid himself, and went out of the temple, going through the midst of them, and so passed by." John 8:59

Quietly, Jesus hid (disguised or altered His appearance so as to be unrecognizable) and walked right through the midst of the crowd. How could He disappear so quickly? This alone should have amazed them, but anger closes the eyes to truth and the heart to faith.

---

[3] These words, "I am that I am," literally is the understanding of the name Jehovah.

The Road to the Cross

Chapter Two

Who Sinned, this Man or His Parents?

Place: Jerusalem - A Sabbath Day at the Temple[1] Time: A Few Weeks Later

Things were too hot around the temple for Jesus to continue His ministry in the temple porches, so He returned to the countryside until things calmed down. It was not yet time to go to the cross. God has a schedule and everything in His plan is always at the right time.

It was the Sabbath day [Saturday], and this morning Jesus and His disciples were on their way to the temple. There would be crowds gathering to hear the teachers in the porches, and of course, 9 AM was sacrifice and prayer time. A blind man was sitting in the vicinity of one of the temple gates. Apparently he was a well-known beggar, as we will see later in the story. This beggar had been blind from birth, and this may have been his favorite spot to beg for alms. It was not permitted for a beggar to beg on the

---

[1] He was in the midst of His final Judean ministry.

Sabbath, but many often went to their spot even on the Sabbath. Sometimes it resulted in some private gift, but at least it reminded the people that they would be there tomorrow.

The pitiful situation of the man aroused empathy in the disciples. One of the disciples asked Jesus, "Who sinned, this man or his parents." They were sure that this terrible tragedy in his life was God's judgment on some sin. It was then, as it often is now, that some imagine that people deserve all the problems or situations that they experience in life. Jesus said that neither had sinned. In reality He was saying that this blindness was not the result of some public or secret sin of his parents or even himself. Jesus was not saying that neither had ever sinned, of course they had, but this was not the result of sin.

> "And his disciples asked him, saying, Master, who did sin, this man, or his parents, that he was born blind? Jesus answered, Neither hath this man sinned, nor his parents: but that the works of God should be made manifest in him." John 9:2-3

What did Jesus mean when He said, *"the works of God should be made manifest in him?"* One of the signs of the Messiah was the ability to heal the blind. It had never been possible before Jesus. When John the Baptist became discouraged during his imprisonment, he sent a delegation to see if Jesus was indeed the Messiah. Jesus said...

> "And John [the, Baptist] calling unto him two of his disciples sent them to Jesus, saying, Art thou he that should come? or look we for another?" Luke 7:19

"Then Jesus answering said unto them, Go your way, and tell John what things ye have seen and heard; how that the blind see, the lame walk, the lepers are cleansed, the deaf hear, the dead are raised, to the poor the gospel is preached." Luke 7:22

How do You Heal a Man Born Blind?

This healing would set both the temple authorities and the Pharisees on their ears. They knew the signs of the Messiah, and they also knew what astonishment such a miracle would have on the people He taught.

No, that isn't the way you heal the blind? You don't put mud in their eyes. You just don't, but Jesus did. He spit on the ground, made a paste, and touched it to his eyes.[2] Then He said, "go wash in the pool of Siloam." The blind man went and washed and he came out seeing.

We learn a very interesting thing in the healing of this young man. The Synagogue had passed a new rule [see the bold type in the verse below]...

"But the Jews did not believe concerning him, that he had been blind, and received his sight, until they called the parents of him that had received his sight. And they asked them, saying, Is this your son, who ye say was born blind? how then doth he now see? His parents answered them and said, We know that this is our son, and that he was born blind: But by what means he now seeth, we know not; or who hath opened his eyes, we know not: he is of age; ask him: he shall speak for himself. These words spake his parents, because they feared the Jews: **for the Jews**

---

[2] Believe it or not, this was a home remedy for those with weak eyes. It may have encouraged the man, but the miracle was the work of Jesus.

> **had agreed already, that if any man did confess that he was Christ, he should be put out of the synagogue.** Therefore said his parents, He is of age; ask him." John 9:18-23

The authorities could not hide the fact that a miracle had occurred among them, the man himself being a chief witness. All they could do was make every attempt to discredit Jesus. How did they do that? By using the Sabbath day. A miracle occurred that had not been done from the beginning of the world, a miracle that only God could do. A man born with blinded eyes was given sight. He was free of the darkness he had sat in so long, free from being a beggar, and free to see all that God had made. All they could think about was not a violation of God's Word. Jesus never violated it; He often crossed the Talmud,[3] which in this case, forbid the healing of a person on the Sabbath. God had said no such thing in His Word.

> "Therefore said some of the Pharisees, This man is not of God, because he keepeth not the **Sabbath day**. Others said, How can a man that is a sinner do such miracles? And there was a division among them." John 9:16

In a private meeting, the young man was saved and worshipped Jesus.

---

[3] The Talmud was a collect of Jewish writers and interpreters containing interpretations, wisdom, and legends. Jesus called it the tradition of man and believed that it clearly violated the Scripture itself. (Matthew 15:6)

The Good Shepherd

Jesus preaches His great sermon on the good Shepherd, clearly identifying Himself with the Shepherd of Psalm twenty-three and announcing that the good shepherd would give His life for His sheep. Jesus announces His death and resurrection, clearly the apostles and disciples should have been prepared for that event that was coming in just six months.

> "I am the good shepherd, and know my sheep, and am known of mine. As the Father knoweth me, even so know I the Father: and I lay down my life for the sheep. And other sheep I have, which are not of this fold: them also I must bring, and they shall hear my voice; and there shall be one fold, and one shepherd. Therefore doth my Father love me, because I lay down my life, that I might take it again. No man taketh it from me, but I lay it down of myself. I have power to lay it down, and I have power to take it again. This commandment have I received of my Father." John 10:14-18

Chapter Three

The Seventy Sent out to Preach

Jesus chooses seventy unnamed disciples and blankets the Judean area with the Gospel message. He gave them power over demons and all manner of sickness. Not only did He give them a broad spectrum of power, but He assigned the authority that is given to all His "sent ones."

> "He that heareth you heareth me; and he that despiseth you despiseth me; and he that despiseth me despiseth him that sent me." Luke 10:16

When they returned rejoicing over the success of their ministry, Jesus quietly said...

> "Notwithstanding in this rejoice not, that the spirits are subject unto you; but rather rejoice, because your names are written in heaven." Luke 10:20

Needless to say, these men preaching in pairs throughout the countryside had reached many people. The popularity of Jesus was growing and so was the rage of the high priests and the Pharisees.

They were ready to take action against Jesus, but they just didn't know what to do. His popularity with the people made them afraid to do any thing rash, so they bided their time but they had already decided that they must do something to stop this new Messiah.

The Road to the Cross

Chapter Four

The Final Miles on the Road to the Cross

The last months of Jesus' earthly ministry began in Jerusalem on 25 Chisleu [December] AD 29 and ended on His return there on Wednesday 14 Nisan [April] AD 30. During those three plus months, we will follow the conclusion of Jesus' last Judean ministry and join in His great Perea ministry. Perea was on the other side of Jordan and also had a village named Bethany. We will follow with Jesus as He receives the news from Martha and Mary that Lazarus was very ill and wanted Jesus to return to Bethany.

The Festival of Lights

Place: Jerusalem   Date: 25 Chisleu AD 29

Winter had come to the land of Judea. It would be cold in Jerusalem and a little snow would fall, while only seven miles or so down the steep mountainside lay the tropical paradise of Jordan basking in the hot sun. The city of Jericho lay deep within the Jordan riff; it was always warm or hot in the valley. These were the days of Hanukkah and pilgrims had been gathering for days now. This festival would mark the beginning of the end of the earthly ministry of Jesus.

Jerusalem was aglow with the great Festival of Light[1] (Hanukkah). The festival was celebrated by the chanting of the Hallel.[2] It was cold in Jerusalem. The chill of the morning wind from the Mediterranean might bring a skiff of snow, so Jesus sought shelter in Solomon's porch, a huge edifice that was adjacent to the temple. This great open structure supported by huge columns offered shelter and a place for crowds to gather for fellowship and religious activities. It was a place of beauty and reflection. The Rabbis[3] and Scribes[4] often held classes within its great confines and visitors often stopped and listened, and if they chose to, they could participate in the Scripture under discussion.

---

[1] Hanukkah was the celebration of the cleansing of the temple and the miracle of the temple lamp that burned eight days on one day's supply of oil. The festival originated in 164 BC after Judas Maccabees restored the temple. It was celebrated for eight days beginning on 25 Chisleu (December).

[2] The word Hallel means *praise*. It denotes the Psalms 113-118, which were chanted in the temple and in the homes during the days of Hanukkah and Passover.

[3] A Rabbi was a Jewish scholar and teacher. Many would be found in the temple area teaching Jewish students. Even those who were just visiting were welcome in the classes.

[4] The Scribes might be from almost any sect of the Jews. It seems that they bound themselves together in a kind of guild. They were those appointed or chosen to hand copy the Scriptures. They were known for accuracy in copying the Scriptures, following diligent rules guaranteeing each copy was an accurate one. Because they copied the Scriptures also called the law, they became experts in their knowledge of where things were in the Scriptures. You might consider them the concordances of the day. They were reverenced for their quick knowledge of the contents of the Scriptures; however, their interpretation of the text was all too often wrong.

Chapter Five

Jesus, a Boy on Solomon's Porch

Place: Jerusalem - The Temple Date: Nisan AD 18

Time: Passover Season

This porch was not new to Jesus. It was on this great porch just over twenty years ago that the twelve year old boy named Jesus, both challenged the teachers and answered their questions to the amazement of all.

> "And it came to pass, that after three days they found him in the temple, sitting in the midst of the doctors, both hearing them, and asking them questions. And all that heard him were astonished at his understanding and answers." Luke 2:46-47

The time in Jerusalem had sped by and Joseph and Mary had started back home to Nazareth assuming that Jesus was traveling with the other boys His age. When the travelers stopped for the night, can you imagine Joseph and Mary's concern and fears when they couldn't find Jesus? By this time there were other children in the family of Joseph and Mary. We know that there were at least six others besides Jesus. There is absolutely no reason not to believe that each of these were the sons of Joseph and Mary, and therefore a half brother or sister to Jesus.

> "Is not this the carpenter's son? is not his mother called Mary? and his brethren, James, and Joses, and Simon, and Judas? And his sisters, are they not all with us?" Matthew 13:55-56a

Had the youngest of the other children been left in the care of a relative or friend at Nazareth? We aren't given that information; some may have been too small to travel with the group while the older children may have been with them.

As the morning light peeped over the hills of Perea, Joseph and Mary were already on their way back to Jerusalem. Asking all the questions a parent asks themselves. Where was that boy? Was He all right? Where did He spend the night? Was He frightened, being in a strange city alone? Like normal parents, they probably made the trip back in record time and began their search. Did they have friends in the city? If they did, they probably searched there first.

The search went on another full day and Jesus was nowhere to be found. Then came another sleepless night for Mary and Joseph. The sun came up from the hills of Moab in the east and they must have went to the temple at the first prayer hour, 9 AM, and to their surprise, there was Jesus sitting and talking with the teachers on Solomon's porch. This had been three exciting days for Jesus, but three agonizing days for His earthly parents. Mary rebuked Him sharply only to be quietly reminded of His mission on earth.

> "And he said unto them, How is it that ye sought me? wist ye not that I must be about my Father's business? And they understood not the saying which he spake unto them. And he went down with them, and came to Nazareth, and was subject unto them: but his mother kept all these sayings in her heart." Luke 2:49-51

While in Jerusalem, the family may have celebrated Jesus' Bar-Mitz, where He became a son of the Covenant. He could take His place with the men in the synagogue. He was even now preparing for that great mission for which He had come, *"To seek and save the lost."*

The scholars and teachers probably never knew what they had missed those days on the porch. They were talking with the Creator of the Universe, God in the flesh, what great wisdom they missed!

> "Now his parents went to Jerusalem every year at the feast of the passover. And when they had fulfilled the days, as they returned, the child Jesus tarried behind in Jerusalem; and Joseph and his mother knew not of it. But they, supposing him to have been in the company, went a day's journey; and they sought him among their kinsfolk and acquaintance. And when they found him not, they turned back again to Jerusalem, seeking him. And it came to pass, that after three days they found him in the temple, sitting in the midst of the doctors, both hearing them, and asking them questions. And all that heard him were astonished at his understanding and answers." Luke 2:41&43-47

Chapter Six

A Different Day on Solomon's Porch

Place: Back in Jerusalem Date: AD 29

It was cold that December morning in Jerusalem, and in the cold of the morning Jesus had just been walking on the great porch of Solomon. Only one or two of His disciples had joined Him, perhaps it was John and Peter. Suddenly, the Jews surrounded Jesus.[1]

They came with a challenge. "Don't leave us in doubt," they said, "if you are the Messiah (Christ), tell us plainly." But did they really want to know so they could believe or did they want to know so they could destroy Him? The latter was probably utmost in their hard hearts and cold minds.

[1] John did not use this title to suggest that all Jews felt the same way about Jesus, apparently they did not. Many believed in Him and others held Him in high esteem, even John and all the disciples were Jews. When John uses the term, he uses it to denote those in leadership - the priests, Pharisees, Sadducees, scribes, the political group called the Herodians, and all the people that actively supported them.

The report of the miracles of Jesus had raised serious questions among the Jews. A notable miracle had been performed in this very vicinity just two months ago. This miracle was considered a definite sign of the Messiah; however, some were disappointed that the miracle was performed on a Sabbath day.

Now at the Festival of Lights, also called the Feast of the Dedication[2] [John 10:22], certain of the Jews confronted Jesus with a stirring question.

> "Then came the Jews round about him, and said unto him, How long dost thou make us to doubt? If thou be the Christ, tell us plainly." John 10:24

Jesus now tells them in no uncertain terms, "I have told you but you did not believe me. You have seen the works that I have done by my Father's authority and they bear witness to whom I am." Most of them would turn their thoughts back two months to the Feast of the Tabernacles in Jerusalem, and how Jesus had opened the eyes of one born blind. This truly was a sign of the Messiah. No one had ever done that before.[3]

Jesus now said that He gave His followers eternal life and they should never perish nor could they be plucked from His Father's

---

[2] The feast was also called the Feast of Dedication because it was on the occasion that the temple was rededicated after its pollution by Antiochus Epiphanes.

[3] Since the world began, it was not heard of that any man had opened the eyes of one that was born blind. If this man were not of God, he could do nothing. John 9:32-33

hand. He had just equated Himself with God the Father as God the Son.

Jesus had just touched a sacred doctrine of Judaism called the *Shema.*

> "Hear, O Israel: The LORD our God is one LORD:" Deuteronomy 6:4. [4]

Jesus had just declared that He was God, what anger flooded their souls! Immediately they sought and picked up stones to stone this great blasphemer. "For which good work do you stone me? Was it the healing two months ago? Or something else I did?" They gave Him the answer...

> "Because that thou, being a man, makest thyself God." John 10:33c

It was perhaps the concluding statements at the end of this conversation that spurred the Pharisees into action. But Jesus roiled them even further, when He said...

> "If I do not the works of my Father, believe me not. But if I do, though ye believe not me, believe the works: that ye may know, and believe, that the Father is in me, and I in him." John 10:37-38

[4] The Christian Trinitarian belief explains the unity of one God. There is indeed one God, but in the unity of that Godhead there are three separate distinguishable persons of the exact same attributes, power, and eternity, whom we know as God the Father, God the Son, and God the Holy Ghost.

"Say ye of him, whom the Father hath sanctified, and sent into the world, Thou blasphemest; because I said, I am the Son of God? If I do not the works of my Father, believe me not. But if I do, though ye believe not me, believe the works: that ye may know, and believe, that the Father is in me, and I in him." John 10:36-38

Stone Him

Now they were determined to stone Jesus, but to do so, they must first drag Him from the confines of Solomon's porch outside the city gate. Their hands already held stones, but before they could be cast, they must first capture Him. But for all their efforts, He escaped out of their hands and was gone from the temple area. How He escaped we are not told, but that He did, we know to be true.

"Then the Jews took up stones again to stone him." John 10:31

"Therefore they sought again to take him: but he escaped out of their hand," John 10:39

Chapter Seven

Dinner at Martha and Mary's

Place: Bethany Date: The Same Day in Chisleu AD 29

Escaping the mob in the temple, Jesus made His way down the little road that began just outside the temple area. Reaching the fork of the road, which went one way to Bethphage and the other to Bethany, He turn Himself and His disciples toward the little suburb of Bethany.[1]

Here Jesus had precious and prestigious friends, and He would be welcome. Martha, who was older, was the head of the house. Was she a widow or just the oldest, who exercised authority in the home possibly after the death of her parents? Lazarus was without any doubt, the young brother of the two women. Mary would have been the middle child. Neither a husband of Martha, nor a father or

[1] Some place this supper in Bethany immediately after the return of the seventy, but it seems to better fit the story at this place. Some harmonies of the Gospel place it here.

mother of the three was mentioned; therefore, we can assume if there had been a husband he was dead and so were the parents.

Arriving sometime in the late afternoon, Martha made Jesus and His disciples welcome, and begin to prepare an elaborate meal for their distinguished guests. It was at this meal that we find Martha complaining because Mary was not helping with the occasion.

All too often food becomes more important than preaching or teaching. The problem did not lie with Mary, who sat at Jesus' feet, but with the spirit within Martha. She had worried herself with something she deemed of the greater importance, while neglecting the greater duty of hearing God's Word.

It was probably at this supper, as she sat listening at the feet of Jesus, that Mary realized the reality of Jesus' soon coming death. At the next occasion, which was a little more than three months away, where Martha was in charge of serving a supper at Simon the Leper's house, Mary anointed Jesus with costly spikenard for His coming death.

> "Now it came to pass, as they went, that he entered into a certain village: and a certain woman named Martha received him into her house. And she had a sister called Mary, which also sat at Jesus' feet, and heard his word. But Martha was cumbered about much serving, and came to him, and said, Lord, dost thou not care that my sister hath left me to serve alone? bid her therefore that she help me. And Jesus answered and said unto her, Martha, Martha, thou art careful and troubled about many things: But one thing is needful: and Mary hath chosen that good part, which shall not be taken away from her." Luke 10:38-42

The Second Giving of the Lord's Prayer

Place: Somewhere in Bethany Time: The Next Morning

Jesus had retired with His disciples for a time of prayer. When one of the disciples asked Jesus to teach them to pray, the Lord's prayer is repeated. Now we fully understand that this isn't the Lord's prayer, it is merely a title given to it.

Jesus encouraged prayer by teaching and by His personal devotional practice. Here, He gives most of the same things in Matthew, which contains the full form of the prayer and leaves out some. However, he will teach them that their heavenly Father makes no mistakes in hearing and answering prayer and gives no bogus gifts. He said...

> "How much more shall your heavenly Father give the Holy Spirit to them that ask him? Luke 11:13b

Of course, they would not now understand this great yet simple truth, but later they would know. God wants to be a part of every part of your life. If you want Him along with you, just ask. This has nothing to do with the abiding of the indwelling of the Holy Spirit, but rather with His conscious presence with you.

Chapter Eight

Retirement into Perea

Place: Leaving Bethany near Jerusalem for Perea Date: Tebeth - Adar AD 30

> "And went away again beyond Jordan into the place where John at first baptized; and there he abode. And many resorted unto him, and said, John did no miracle: but all things that John spake of this man were true. And many believed on him there." John 10:40-42

Leaving Bethany, we move with Jesus and His disciples northeast down past Jericho and into the land of Perea. The territory lay east of the Jordan, outside the jurisdiction of the priests and the temple authority at Jerusalem. We know that it was a full day's foot journey from Bethany, and the fellow that had made that one-day journey to Perea had come on urgent business. Likely, it took Jesus and His disciples, traveling leisurely, the better part of two days.

There was a little village near the Jordan River in an area where John the Baptist once baptized. The village was called Bethany, and is often confused with the Bethany near Jerusalem where Mary,

Martha, and Lazarus lived. The location of this village is unknown today. Some have suggested that this little city became Jesus' headquarters for the three months between Chisleu (December) and Adar (March).

Here in Perea, many resorted to Jesus. They came to hear Him because they had confidence in two things, the testimony of John the Baptist, for Perea had once been his headquarters, and the fact that although John had performed no miracle, everything he had said about this man [Jesus] was true. Many believed in Him in Perea.

Even Perea was not beyond the reach of the sect of the Pharisees, which was by large the most popular of the religious sects of the Jews. Their separation and belief in the Scriptures and their devotion to the Talmud, the book of traditions, had given to them a position in religion. But they were bitter enemies of Jesus and sought on every occasion to discredit and destroy His image before the people. They were here in Perea too, and would attack Jesus on any and every possible occasion. They were, with their actions, creating the final confrontation.

Healing a Woman on the Sabbath in Perea

Place: Perea, East of Jordan | Date: Early in Tebeth AD 30

> "And he was teaching in one of the synagogues on the sabbath. And, behold, there was a woman which had a spirit of infirmity eighteen years, and was bowed together, and could in no wise lift

up herself. And when Jesus saw her, he called her to him, and said unto her, Woman, thou art loosed from thine infirmity. And he laid his hands on her: and immediately she was made straight, and glorified God. And the ruler of the synagogue answered with indignation, because that Jesus had healed on the sabbath day, and said unto the people, There are six days in which men ought to work: in them therefore come and be healed, and not on the sabbath day. The Lord then answered him, and said, Thou hypocrite, doth not each one of you on the sabbath loose his ox or his ass from the stall, and lead him away to watering? And ought not this woman, being a daughter of Abraham, whom Satan hath bound, lo, these eighteen years, be loosed from this bond on the sabbath day? And when he had said these things, all his adversaries were ashamed: and all the people rejoiced for all the glorious things that were done by him. Then said he, Unto what is the kingdom of God like? and whereunto shall I resemble it? It is like a grain of mustard seed, which a man took, and cast into his garden; and it grew, and waxed a great tree; and the fowls of the air lodged in the branches of it. And again he said, Whereunto shall I liken the kingdom of God? It is like leaven, which a woman took and hid in three measures of meal, till the whole was leavened." Luke 13:10-21

Luke tells us that Jesus taught in a synagogue[1] in Perea on the Sabbath day, and there was a woman, who was so ill that she could not straighten up but walked in a stooped position. We are not told what her illness was, but doctor Luke was always aware of symptoms and what they did to the body. In one act of mercy, Jesus healed her, but it was on the Sabbath. Jesus took no stock in how the ancient rabbi had interpreted the command to observe the Sabbath. Many were the occasions, when He deliberately disregarded them to perform His ministry.

---

[1] The synagogues started during the captivity of Judah in the land of Babylon. It is believed that Ezekiel began them when he taught the people in the land of Babylon. Their purpose was the ministry of teaching and preaching the Word of God. They were scattered throughout the land of Israel and wherever there was enough Jewish men to begin one.

Immediately a challenge came from the ruler of the synagogue. Why? Because it was the Sabbath. Jesus then gave the whole congregation a sermon on why it was permitted to do right on the Sabbath and relieve human suffering. Using the poor woman as an example, Jesus put His adversaries to shame and won the hearts of those who heard Him.

Chapter Nine

A Brief Return to Judea

Place: From Perea back to Judea Date: Early Tebeth AD 30

> "And he went through the cities and villages, teaching, and journeying toward Jerusalem. Then said one unto him, Lord, are there few that be saved? And he said unto them, Strive to enter in at the strait gate: for many, I say unto you, will seek to enter in, and shall not be able. When once the master of the house is risen up, and hath shut to the door, and ye begin to stand without, and to knock at the door, saying, Lord, Lord, open unto us; and he shall answer and say unto you, I know you not whence ye are:" Luke 13:22-35

This had been in the unannounced plans of Jesus all along. Remember He had sent the seventy out to all the villages that He had planned to visit, and now He is accomplishing His mission in visiting those very villages. Although the plan to visit them was unpublished, His enemies were everywhere these days and soon they would meet Him by chance or design. The whole plan seemed to be to end the tour in Jerusalem.

As they traveled, someone in the crowd asked Jesus, "Are there few that be saved?" Those following Jesus seemed dwarfed by the opposition. To answer, Jesus said...

> "Strive to enter in at the strait[1] gate: for many, I say unto you, will seek to enter in, and shall not be able." Luke 13:24

There would come a time when they would desire to be saved; however, it would be too late, for the door would be shut to them forever.

That very day, there came a group of Pharisees warning Him to get out of the country. I seriously doubt if they cared, but the warning did sound serious enough. Herod had killed John the Baptist, and Jesus may have been somewhere near Herod's jurisdiction.

Jesus' time and place of death was no accident. Herod would not determine the time of His death, which had been predetermined in the great plan of God. Until that time, Jesus assured them that He would continue His ministry. The terms that He must walk today, tomorrow, and the day following indicated, not now but at the proper time that the Prophet will perish in Jerusalem.

> "Nevertheless I must walk to day, and to morrow, and the day following: for it cannot be that a prophet perish out of Jerusalem." Luke 13:33

---

[1] A strait is a very narrow passage; of course the only way into salvation is narrow and exclusive. Jesus said, "No man commeth to the Father, but by me."

Jesus Weeps over Jerusalem

Place: Mount of Olives Date: Middle or End of Tebeth AD 30

> "O Jerusalem, Jerusalem, which killest the prophets, and stonest them that are sent unto thee; how often would I have gathered thy children together, as a hen doth gather her brood under her wings, and ye would not! Behold, your house is left unto you desolate: and verily I say unto you, Ye shall not see me, until the time come when ye shall say, Blessed is he that cometh in the name of the Lord." Luke 13:34-35

> "O Jerusalem, Jerusalem, thou that killest the prophets, and stonest them which are sent unto thee, how often would I have gathered thy children together, even as a hen gathereth her chickens under her wings, and ye would not! Behold, your house is left unto you desolate. For I say unto you, Ye shall not see me henceforth, till ye shall say, Blessed is he that cometh in the name of the Lord." Matthew 23:37-39

The roadway to the eastern gate of the city of Jerusalem wound lazily down the Mount of Olives. Near the peak of Mount Olivet, the temple located on the side of Zion's hill opened to the view of the traveler. One could look over the walls into the temple courts and see the activities. It must have been from this vantage point that Jesus spoke the next two verses.

> "O Jerusalem, Jerusalem, which killest the prophets, and stonest them that are sent unto thee; how often would I have gathered thy children together, as a hen doth gather her brood under her wings, and ye would not! Behold, your house is left unto you desolate: and verily I say unto you, Ye shall not see me, until the time come when ye shall say, Blessed is he that cometh in the name of the Lord." Luke 13:34-35

Jerusalem and the nation had rejected the prophets of God, ignored God's call, and refused His care. He had tried to offer them the shelter of His protective wings, lovingly calling them as a hen clucks for her chicks to come to the shelter of her spread wings, and yet they would not come. When love, mercy, and grace have been refused, the only thing that remains is judgment. In these verses, Jesus is abandoning Jerusalem and the temple to the coming judgment of God. It is a heart-breaking message that tore at the heart of Jesus.

The Road to the Cross

Chapter Ten

Returning to Perea

Place: Perea, East of Jordan Date: Late in Tebeth AD 30

Reference: Luke 14:1-24

Leaving Jerusalem, we take the road down toward the Jordan depression, crossing over Jordan near Gilgal and heading up into Perea. Sometime after arriving among the villages, Jesus is invited to have a Sabbath meal with the chief of the Pharisees in the area. Of course, others have gathered for this important occasion, among them is a lawyer [a Scribe]. They were ready for a religious argument.

Jesus knew the hearts of men and knew this would be an unfriendly meeting at best. He gave them every opportunity to do the right thing. An unknown man came to breakfast; this was an open practice. Anyone could drop in for the dinner conversation and possibly leftovers. This man was in the advanced stages of dropsy;[1] swollen hands and feet would announce the extent of his disease.

More and more this was looking like a set up. Jesus had healed a woman on the Sabbath a few weeks ago, and now they had their own test case. Jesus knew their thoughts and Himself raised the question on their minds, *"Is it lawful to heal on the Sabbath day?"*

The Pharisees were very strict about the Sabbath. Well, they did cut it thin when it came to themselves. They often had elaborate meals on the Sabbath, preparing the food for the festival the day before; however, it seems to me that serving the feast would have constituted as work for the servants.

As He often did, Jesus turned to practical things to illustrate His point.

> "Which of you shall have an ass or an ox fallen into a pit, and will not straightway pull him out on the sabbath day? And they could not answer him again to these things." Luke 14:5b-6

There were two things shown here. One was the loss of money and the other was an act of mercy to animals. They certainly would not want to make a public declaration that would deny a poor farmer the opportunity to save his means of livelihood. But an act of mercy toward a fellow human being on the Sabbath day, well, that

---

[1] This is the only occasion in which Jesus dealt with this disease. In dropsy, bodily fluids gather in the body often filling the lungs, and usually ends in congestive heart failure.

was different. In the letter of the law they had lost the spirit of the law. Jesus had told them earlier...

> "And he said unto them, The sabbath was made for man, and not man for the sabbath: Therefore the Son of man is Lord also of the sabbath." Mark 2:27-28

Lessons in Humility

Place: The Pharisee's Home in Bethany of Perea Date: Tebeth AD 30

Using two different allegories, Jesus politely but firmly rebuked the crowd. They had been busy finding the chief seats and the places of honor at the meal with Jesus. They certainly wanted to shine on this special occasion. What fools they had made of themselves in front of the Son of God.

The other lesson showed the motive behind some invitations. There was the hope of reciprocation lodged deep within the invitations of the host. There was neither humility nor compassion in the actions of the host. Jesus was exposing this meeting for what it was, a gathering of opposition.

The Cost of Discipleship

Reference: Luke 14: 25-35

Opposition was getting stronger and stronger. The Pharisees did not fear the apostles, but they did fear the great crowds that were following Him, and He had made other disciples in Perea. Jesus would not lead the disciples blindly. He made them aware of the crucifixion and the persecution that would surely follow. To be a follower of Jesus would require a certain kind of deep commitment. The disciples must base their commitment in the knowledge of what they might have to endure for Jesus' sake.

Two parables are told to illustrate this. The first is the builder who laid the foundation of a tower before ascertaining whether he could complete the building. The second was the parable about a king going to war, who thought over the engagement and decided that with his smaller forces it was better to send ambassadors to make peace.

Chapter Eleven

The Chapter of Lost Things

Place: Somewhere in the Country of Perea Date: Shebat AD 30

Some publicans and sinners gathered to hear Jesus. Because of their coherence with the Romans in a lucrative tax business, which usually was fraudulent, the tax collectors (publicans) were usually considered to be the outcasts of society. The Pharisees would not have even spoken to them should they have passed them on the street or in the marketplace. They had doomed them to eternal damnation and would not so much as lift a finger for their salvation. In fact, they did not believe that they were worthy to approach God. This is graphically displayed in the story Jesus told about prayer on the road to Jerusalem for the last time.

> "Two men went up into the temple to pray; the one a Pharisee, and the other a publican. The Pharisee stood and prayed thus with himself, God, I thank thee, that I am not as other men are, extortioners, unjust, adulterers, or even as this publican. I fast twice in the week, I give tithes of all that I possess. And the publican, standing afar off, would not lift up so much as his eyes unto heaven, but smote upon his breast, saying, God be merciful to me a sinner. I tell you, this man went down to his house

> justified rather than the other: for every one that exalteth himself shall be abased; and he that humbleth himself shall be exalted." Luke 18:10-14

But, at the feet of Jesus, sinners found a ready welcome. The Pharisees, strict separatists, and the scribes also believed that this showed the true character of Jesus. He must be one of them or He would not be so hospitable to them. So they drew clean robes around dirty hearts and found fault with the One whom Gabriel said had come to save His people from their sins. They found still further fault with Jesus because He not only received people of this character, but actually sat down at the table and took meals with them. How very contaminating this was in the eyes of the religious hypocrites.

Lost - a Sheep, a Coin, and a Son

With three potent stories, Jesus would illustrate the value that God sets upon lost souls. Cloaked in terms they could understand, the master storyteller awoke the soul and challenged the heart of these hardhearted Pharisees and scribes. Their murmuring about His fellowship with the lost had not gone unnoticed.

These three stories reveal the heart and attitude of God the Father. He seeks the lost, waits on the wayward to come home, and tries to reason with those who do not understand His love and compassion.

One Sheep Missing

Lost sheep were a common occurrence in the land of Israel. As they graze with their head down, they soon become separated from the flock. They were subject to all the dangers of the wilderness, including large predators. Each sheep was special to the shepherd; each had a name and a place in the flock. At night when the sheep were brought into the fold, one was missing.

The good shepherd would leave the flock safely in the fold, and spend the night in the wilderness, if necessary, seeking the lost sheep. Now the Pharisees, many which were probably herd owners, could understand that loss and sympathize with the shepherd. In this case, the shepherd's search ended in success, the sheep was found and he carried it home on his shoulder.

Such a find called for a celebration of sorts, so he called his friends and neighbors for a party. They too realize the worth of the sheep and were happy to celebrate the event with him.

Just in case they had missed the whole point of what Jesus had said, Jesus explained the parable to them.

> "I say unto you, that likewise joy shall be in heaven over one sinner that repenteth, more than over ninety and nine just persons, which need no repentance." Luke 15:7

A Missing Coin

A woman had lost a coin, possibly part of her marriage dowry. She would not stop until it was found. She lighted a lamp, swept the floor, and searched until the coin was recovered. It was time for celebration; friends and neighbors were invited, for she had found the coin that was very important to her. Again, Jesus will make His point clear.

> "Likewise, I say unto you, there is joy in the presence of the angels of God over one sinner that repenteth." Luke 15:10

A Son Gone to a Far Country

A rebellious son insulted his father by asking for his inheritance. Taking it with him, he left for a far country. Here in just a short time he had wasted it all with riotous living. In desperation, he was feeding pigs and looking longingly at their food because he was so hungry.

One day while sitting and contemplating his fate, he came to himself and said, "I will arise and go to my father and say, 'Father, I have sinned against heaven and in thy sight, make me a hired servant'." Instead, the father, who had been watching for his return, ran to meet him on the road home. He called for clothing, a ring, and shoes and held a great party. For he said...

> "For this my son was dead, and is alive again; he was lost, and is found. And they began to be merry." Luke 15:24

Jesus' purpose on earth was according to His own words.

> "For the Son of man is come to seek and to save that which was lost." Luke 19:10

Lost in the Land of Self-Righteousness

Of course, in the last half of this parable, Jesus described the Pharisees and scribes. They were much like the older brother. They were moral, industrious, remained at home, and served, but they could not stand those whom they deemed the dregs or failures of life. They were certainly not worthy of association with the elite of God, as they believed themselves to be. There was neither love, kindness, nor grace in their attitude or practice.

The older brother had stayed home and served, but there was not an ounce of compassion in his cold heart. He was filled with his own righteousness. He did not regard the joy of his father or the repentance of the brother as anything that should concern him. The return of his brother was nothing more than a liability to him and a reproach to the family name. He believed in his heart that the father loved the wayward son more than he loved him.

And so it was with the Pharisees and scribes, they neither desired nor sought the salvation of others. Resting in their own self-made righteousness and religious practices, they had no feeling for those who were perishing in their sins.

Chapter Twelve

The Worldly Wise Steward

Place: Perea Date: Sometime in Shebat AD 30

Reference: Luke 16:1-18

Jesus had told this parable to His disciples, but wherever Jesus went these days, there were Pharisees and scribes waiting. Their opposition had intensified, and they were becoming more vocal in that opposition. It was the war of public opinion that they were hoping to win and Jesus was pushing them to the edge.

In the parable, the servant did not become a crook after hearing his master was about to call him into accounting; he was already a dishonest embezzler. Facing certain judgment, he realized his precarious position and made an effort to secure his own future by using his master's money. The dishonest servant quickly realized judgment was at hand. The master was returning and the servant would be required to give an account.

Jesus never commends a crook and neither did He commend this one. The servant's master, whom ever he was, marveled that the servant was so resourceful, even if he did steal from him. Jesus' words are words of rebuke.

God has given you opportunity to use His possessions to provide for eternal life, not to be saved but to lay up treasures in heaven. If a man is not faithful to God in his money, neither will he be faithful in other matters. How a man uses his possessions (money and goods) is a revelation of the manner of individual he really is.

> "He that is faithful in that which is least is faithful also in much: and he that is unjust in the least is unjust also in much. If therefore ye have not been faithful in the unrighteous mammon, who will commit to your trust the true riches?" Luke 16:10-11

Jesus also warned the disciples and those standing nearby of the folly of trying to serve two masters.

> "No servant can serve two masters: for either he will hate the one, and love the other; or else he will hold to the one, and despise the other. Ye cannot serve God and mammon." Luke 16:13

The Pharisees, who prided themselves on the law, accepting the Talmud (the written traditions) with equal authority with the very Word of God, were *covetous.*[1] They literally turned up their nose at the teachings of Christ. Jesus now makes five public statements about the law and the Pharisee's relationship to it.

---

[1] A lover of money.

1. You justify yourselves, but God knows your heart.
2. Some things treasured by man may be hated by God.
3. The law and prophets were unto John the Baptist.
4. Not one tittle[2] of the law will fail.
5. The law does not yield to Rabbi tradition in family relationship.

[2] The smallest stroke identifying a letter in the law.

The Road to the Cross

Chapter Thirteen

Somewhere Between Death and the Life to Come

Reference: Luke 16:19-31

This story is often called a parable; however, it differs from all parables in that a person is named and it does not use the words like or as. Everything is stated in a definite manner.

The story is in an Old Testament setting and naturally will be as things were back then. Since the death, burial, and resurrection of Jesus, Old Testament Paradise[1] and hell have continued to exist until this very hour and will receive the saved and unsaved dead until the second resurrection.[2]

---

[1] Paradise is a Babylonian word that literally means *a garden*. It was a beautiful place of rest until the resurrection of Jesus. It cannot, of course, compare to the beauties of heaven where all the saints, both Old and New Testament rest awaiting the resurrection. Ephesians 4:8-10

[2] There are two resurrections. The first resurrection began with the resurrection of Jesus, continues at His return for His Church, and is complete with the resurrection and translation of the tribulation saints. The second resurrection, which is the resurrection unto damnation (the unsaved), occurs one thousand years later at the Judgment of the Great White Throne.

Lazarus, in failing health and destitute of finances, was just a beggar that lay by the rich man's gate. His body was in grievous shape and none would have wanted to associate with him; however, beyond the sight of man was the forgiveness of God. In the course of life, death comes to all men and death came to the beggar. Unseen by human eyes, angels waited to carry his soul away to Abraham's bosom.[3] Here at rest, he is very soon spotted by an old neighbor.

Despite his wealth, luxury, and power, the rich man too died and was buried. Again unseen to humans, angels awaited his death and he was immediately consigned a place of flames, torment, and pain, known as hell. It seemed to be a lonely place, for we see no other faces and hear no other voices, but multitudes are there even now awaiting that final resurrection and fearful judgment of the Great White Throne.

He made two requests of Abraham. The first was for a bit of moisture from Lazarus's finger and the second was for Lazarus to return and warn his five brothers not to come to this awful place. Hell is the confining place for all those who are lost and who never by grace through faith receive Christ as Saviour.

---

[3] Abraham's bosom meant a place of fellowship with the Father of the faithful, and of course, with all the saints that had arrived earlier. It will be to this Old Testament that the dying thief accompanied Jesus, but it was indeed a short visit, for he was immediately taken up with the rest when Jesus changed the waiting place.

Abraham's final answer...

> "They have Moses and the prophets; let them hear them." Luke 16:29b

Chapter Fourteen

Forgiveness

> "Then said he unto the disciples, It is impossible but that offences will come: but woe unto him, through whom they come! It were better for him that a millstone were hanged about his neck, and he cast into the sea, than that he should offend one of these little ones. Take heed to yourselves: If thy brother trespass against thee, rebuke him; and if he repent, forgive him. And if he trespass against thee seven times in a day, and seven times in a day turn again to thee, saying, I repent; thou shalt forgive him. And the apostles said unto the Lord, Increase our faith. And the Lord said, If ye had faith as a grain of mustard seed, ye might say unto this sycamine tree, Be thou plucked up by the root, and be thou planted in the sea; and it should obey you." Luke 17:1-6

Peter may have raised this question in Matthew 18, when he proposed a set limit on the forgiveness of others. The rabbis taught that three times was sufficient, but Peter would do them one better. He doubled their number and added one, but the ante was upped, Jesus said, *"until seventy times seven."* He also added the illustrating story of the unforgiving servant, who could accept the forgiveness of his great debt from his master, but could not show the same kindness to a brother.

Offenses would come; they are the most severe against the young or immature Christians. We must use care in helping them. However, the world too will attack the believer and leave deep and lasting wounds, but our forgiveness of others must exceed their actions against us. Only this kind of forgiveness can keep bitterness out of the heart of believers.

And our saved brother or sister, how must we forgive him or her? With the grace and help of God. God carefully combines His love with the love we give to others. God bases our duty to forgive upon His great love and forgiveness for us.

> "And be ye kind one to another, tenderhearted, forgiving one another, even as God for Christ's sake hath forgiven you." Ephesians 4:32

Here Jesus turns up the heat on forgiveness by telling the disciples that forgiving others has no end.

> "And if he trespass against thee seven times in a day, and seven times in a day turn again to thee, saying, I repent; thou shalt forgive him." Luke 17:4

The Unprofitable Servant

> "But which of you, having a servant plowing or feeding cattle, will say unto him by and by, when he is come from the field, Go and sit down to meat? And will not rather say unto him, Make ready wherewith I may sup, and gird thyself, and serve me, till I have eaten and drunken; and afterward thou shalt eat and drink? Doth he thank that servant because he did the things that were commanded him? I trow not. So likewise ye, when ye shall have done all those things which are commanded you, say, We are

> unprofitable servants: we have done that which was our duty to do." Luke 17:7-10

What makes one a profitable servant? Jesus illustrated this with a servant who worked all day at his master's bidding in the field. When evening came, he commanded the servant to prepare a meal, since neither had eaten. When the meal was ready, he commanded the servant to serve it. Now at last, the servant could sit down and take his own meal.

Now we would have called that man a good and faithful servant, he did all his master asked or commanded, but he did nothing more. Jesus called the man an unprofitable servant. Why? Because he did not go the extra mile or have any initiative or imagination of his own. Such people treat everything as belonging to another and treat it without either love or desire for improvement. When you serve God, please bring your mind along with your heart, you will need both.

Chapter Fifteen

Messengers Arriving from Judah

Place: Bethany, Perea Date: Sometime in the Last Week of Adar AD 30
Reference: John 11

Lazarus was gravely ill in Bethany, Judea. Of course, all was being done for him that could be done, but the situation grew worse by the hour. Martha and Mary dispatched a runner to find and tell Jesus of their dilemma. They would trust His judgment to do the right thing. The messenger was simply to tell Jesus that his friend Lazarus was sick, and to make him aware that the situation had become very grave.

They probably expected Jesus later the following day; however, before the first day ended Lazarus had expired. Jesus and the disciples went about their work the next two days. On the fourth day, Jesus said, *"Let's go into Judea again."*

The disciples had not forgotten the problems at Jerusalem. They remembered those who had picked up stones to stone Jesus. They thought it a bit dumb to return to a place where every moment you were in jeopardy of your life. One can imagine a thousand questions on why to go back, but Jesus simply said...

> "Our friend Lazarus sleepeth;[1] but I go, that I may wake him out of his sleep." John 11:11b

Well, if he is sleeping, he is doing all right the disciples began to say, but Jesus spoke plainly, *"Lazarus is dead."* Thomas, who seems to be pessimistic in his thinking, suggests that they just all go with Jesus and die with Him. While that seems quite noble at the time, it did not keep Thomas from scattering with most of the other apostles on the night that Jesus was arrested in the Garden of Gethesame.

At the Grave of a Friend

Place: Bethany Judah | Date: First Week of Nisan AD 30

The house of Martha and Mary was filled to the overflowing with guests, which included family, friends, professional mourners, and the ever present, Pharisees, scribes, and spies for the high priests. These spies seemed to be everywhere, always looking for some damning information against Jesus of Nazareth.

---

[1] For the very first time the metaphor sleep is used to denote the death of a believer. Hereafter, it will be used of all believers who die; however, it is never used of the unsaved.

Mourning usually went on for several days, depending on a family's ability to pay for food and refreshments for the mourners. The family was a very well to do family and apparently well known in both Bethany and Jerusalem. Bethany is only fifteen furlongs (1.7 miles) from Jerusalem and was more like a suburb than a separate city.

Lazarus had died from causes not explained; however, death had followed only a few days of illness. Martha and Mary believed that Jesus would come for His friend Lazarus and for their sake, so they had sent for Him. This family's faith in Christ was so intense that when Jesus arrived in the village on the evening of the fourth day after Lazarus' death, Martha went out of the house to meet and greet Jesus saying...

> "if thou [Jesus] had been here, my brother had not died. But I know, that even now, whatsoever thou wilt ask of God, God will give it thee." John 11:21b-22

Martha's faith in Christ remained undaunted despite the loss of her younger brother, Lazarus. Her words, although they seemed to be a mild rebuke for not coming earlier, were rather an expression of her warm and glowing faith in Christ. Mary, the other sister, had remained in the house although she also knew that Jesus had arrived. She had always been the more spiritual one, yet now she seemed to be the most disappointed and depressed.

Jesus requested to be taken to the gravesite, which Martha and Mary were glad to do. They were followed by disciples, mourners, and skeptics. Why didn't this man who opened the eyes of the blind do something so that Lazarus would not have died? It seems that they were remembering the event from last October when the man born blind was healed.

Lord, He's Been Dead Four Days

Place: Bethany, Outside the City Walls

The family gravesite would probably have been just beyond the city walls and may have been in a garden since they were able to afford it. The burial place was either a prepared cave or a hued opening in a solid limestone wall.

As Jesus, Martha, and Mary, followed by the disciples and their guests, walked through the winding streets of the little village to the gravesite others joined them. The evening was casting large shadows on the ground, for the sun was hovering near the western horizon.

There was quite a crowd in the graveyard. Pausing for a moment, Jesus wept. His heart was a sympathetic heart, feeling all the grief that Martha and Mary must have been through these last four days. Despite their doubts and concerns, they had doggedly held on to their faith that Jesus was indeed the true Messiah sent to Israel.

No one seemed to know what to expect on this occasion. Some in the group may have heard of the raising of the widow's son at Nain or Jairus' daughter at Capernaum; however, the time between their death and their restoration to life had only been a few hours. This time it had been four days.[2] Maybe all these accounts of raising the dead had been purely fictional; they happened a long ways from Jerusalem and who had seen them?

Remove the Stone

Evening shadows made the sealed tomb look ominous and forbearing. Roll away the stone? Jesus, you should reconsider this request for the opening of Lazarus' tomb. He has now been dead for four days and the tomb would be filled with the horrible stench of decaying flesh. Martha would say...

> "Lord, by this time he stinketh: for he hath been dead four days."
> John 11:39b

At Jesus insistence, strong men rushed forward to remove the heavy stone closing the mouth of the tomb. Stones used to close the graves were usually hewed from the soft limestone and were either rolled or set into place. Quickly, the stone was set aside. Nothing moved in the stillness of the dark tomb, which was made even darker by the evening shadows.

[2] Jewish tradition said that the spirit stayed within the body for three consecutive days following their death. Remember that it is tradition and not a Bible truth. However, Jesus would raise Lazarus despite their beliefs.

To Martha, Jesus said...

> "Said I not unto thee, that, if thou wouldest believe, thou shouldest see the glory of God?" John 11:40b

Jesus after this short prayer, which was for those standing around that they might see that God had sent Him, called Lazarus from the tomb. Note that He carefully specified whom He wanted, for had He generalized whom He wanted up from the dead, there could have been all the dead raised.

"*Lazarus come forth.*" There in the deep shadows of the doorway stood Lazarus, bound in the Jewish grave clothing. It was almost impossible for Lazarus to walk, and until his hand were free, he could not remove the grave cloth from his face. Jesus commands them to remove the grave clothing and free Lazarus.

Joy and awe must have overcome Martha and Mary. Their brother who was dead these four days was alive again. They had come to the gravesite with deep sorrow and grief and were returned home rejoicing in the Lord. Lazarus had been fully restored to life.[3] This was a convincing display of the omnipotent powers of Christ and many there believe on Jesus.

---

[3] The raising of the dead was a return to natural life with all its limitations. The person would die again at some later date. It is improper to call this a resurrection. Jesus would be the very first person ever to be resurrected.

The Road to the Cross

Chapter Sixteen

Jesus Puts Pressure on His Enemies

From late September AD 29 to April AD 30, Jesus relentlessly kept the pressure on the religious authorities around Jerusalem, through His miracles and by His teaching. Jesus had slowly and surely backed His enemies into the corner. He was forcing a choice upon them. They must either acknowledge Him as the Son of God and therefore, the Messiah of Israel or they must destroy Him. For the first time the groups united in their purpose. They would first try to destroy Him by discrediting His work, but the miracles were undeniable. Then they attempted to cast suspicion on His person and when that failed they resorted to the final solution, kill Him. But they must do it cautiously so they could protect their positions and their images before the people.

What they were planning was premeditated murder. What Jesus made it to be was the sacrificial offering of Himself for our sins.

The Plot

Place: Jerusalem, Sanhedrin Room in the Temple Date: The Next Day AD 30
Time: Sundown

Those friendly with the high priests and the Pharisees rushed out into the coming darkness, they had powerful and urgent news. Lazarus of Bethany, who had been dead for four days, was restored to life by Jesus from Galilee. It happened in front of a multitude of witnesses, and there was no easy way to discredit this miracle.

This latest incident was too much, it brought instant reaction. First, it was a notable miracle. Secondly, it had been witnessed by a vast number of witnesses. Finally, it had been performed practically on the doorstep of the temple. This called for an immediate meeting of the executive committee tonight. They must plan and plot their course of action. The very words of the council denoted the seriousness of the moment.

> "Then gathered the chief priests and the Pharisees a council, and said, **What do we? for this man doeth many miracles. If we let him thus alone, all men will believe on him: and the Romans shall come and take away both our place and nation.** And one of them, named Caiaphas, being the high priest that same year, said unto them, Ye know nothing at all, Nor consider that it is expedient for us, that one man should die for the people, and that the whole nation perish not." John 11:47-50

The council reached a terrible decision that dark night, for they agreed together to put Jesus to death. They were planning a way to accomplish this very feat without jeopardizing their position or endangering their present political position with the Romans. The Romans basically left the temple area alone.

Caiaphas and Annas ran a very lucrative business in the money exchange. They forced pilgrims to change their currency into acceptable temple money and buy approved animals for sacrifice. Everything was sold at several times the true market value. These booths were often referred to as the "booths of Annas." They accounted for much of the wealth of the high priests family.

Most, if not all, of the sect of the Pharisees were in complete agreement with the executive decision that Caiaphas, the acting high priest, and the council had made. The priestly groups were all Sadducees. Normally the two groups were miles apart, and doctrinally that did not change, but they all agreed on the need to destroy Jesus.

Normally, the two Jewish sects had no dealings with one another, radically differing greatly on the fundamentals of their faith. The Pharisees held to the authority of all the Scriptures; the Sadducees only to the Pentateuch, even doubting some of that. They differed on the resurrection of the dead. The Sadducees denied the resurrection, the judgments, and the after life, while the Pharisees believed them to be true.

They both, however, rejected Jesus' claim as Messiah. He just did not meet their expectations. Who was this nobody from Nazareth, who had moved the populace with His words and His miracles? He was not one of them, He had not come from Jerusalem, and He did not have the sanction of the important people. Jesus would challenge them with His works, His miracles, and the Scriptures themselves. He said, "They testify [bear witness] of me." Their petty religion was under a threat. The high priest spoke prophetically at the gathering, though I am sure he did not mean to.

> "And one of them, named Caiaphas, being the high priest that same year, said unto them, Ye know nothing at all, Nor consider that it is expedient for us, that one man should die for the people, and that the whole nation perish not. And this spake he not of himself: but being high priest that year, **he prophesied that Jesus should die for that nation; And not for that nation only, but that also he should gather together in one the children of God that were scattered abroad.** Then from that day forth they took counsel together for to put him to death." John 11:49-53

It was not the spiritual outlook that Caiaphas had under consideration, it was the fear of the Roman authorities. They mingled too much already with the temple and religion. The priests had a good thing going at the temple, it was profitable, very religious, and they were in favor. The Pharisees on the other hand could not abide Jesus' teaching and His insistence on inward conversion before outward profession.

Minutes from the Sanhedrin Executive Meeting

Place: Jerusalem, Sanhedrin Room in the Temple

The Sanhedrin convened, though not all members were present. It is doubtful that even a quorum was present. This was an emergency. When events happened in Nain, Nazareth, Cana, or even Capernaum, it was far away and under another jurisdiction, that of Herod Agrippa. This was Jerusalem and it happened under the very nose of the authorities. That man blind from birth had been healed at the vicinity of the temple and now Lazarus of Bethany, a man of means and influence, had been raised from the dead in the presence of many witnesses. It was an emergency of enormous proportion as far as they were concerned. I doubt if they kept minutes of this session, but God did. They reached the following conclusions...

(1) The miracles of Jesus could not be easily refuted and they had made him very popular among the people.

(2) Because of the miracles all men would believe on Him.

(3) This popularity would, at least in their belief, trigger the Romans into believing that Jesus was indeed the long awaited King of Israel. The Messiah of God was sent to set up the throne of David in Jerusalem. Any notion of rebellion was met with swift and sudden military action by the Romans. They would shut down Jerusalem and stop the crowds that always streamed into its gates. It could be serious enough to lose their national identity. The Romans had always overreacted to even the suggestion of rebellion. They could remember the crucifixion of hundreds of rebels in the past. The roadway had been lined with their crosses and the winds carried their agonizing cries. The non-patriotic priests did not want that to happen again, in fact, they were not willing to take a chance on it.

(4) They resolved and committed themselves to put Jesus to death.

The Road to the Cross

Chapter Seventeen

Jesus Leaves Judah Heading North

Place: Jerusalem, Two Days Following the Decision of the Sanhedrin to Kill Jesus

The high priests and Pharisees must use caution in their attack on Jesus, and an even greater caution, if they make any attempt at killing Him. While they were still forming their plans, Jesus and His disciples left Jerusalem and headed in the direction of Galilee.

After saying their good-byes in Bethany, Jesus and His disciples took the road north into Samaria. The authorities would think that He was headed back to His headquarters in Capernaum. Jerusalem was a seething danger pot; both He and His disciples would have been in grave danger anywhere in the city. Prior to Passover there would have been only a few Galileans in the city and the priests would have no fear of rioting should they arrest Jesus. Besides, Pilate had returned back to his headquarters in the Roman city of Caesarea, leaving the priest with pretty much a free hand. Leaving Jerusalem was a very good idea.

It was not yet time for the cross, that must come at the Festival of Passover and it was still days away. They would be safe in the northern country where Jesus was more popular. But Jesus did not go to the large city; instead He would rest in the little village of Ephraim at the northern border between Samaria and Galilee some twenty or twenty-five miles north of Jerusalem. It would be a quiet and restful time before the coming days of great stress at Jerusalem.

Within a day or so, Jesus moved even farther north on the edge of the Samaritan border to the city of Beth shan[1] (Scythopolis). The city set along a small stream not far from the Jordan River and became the staging point for His final trip to Jerusalem for the Passover and the cross.

---

[1] Beth shan was the city where the Philistines took the dead bodies of Saul and Jonathan and displayed them on the wall after the battle of Mt. Gilboa. The bodies were rescued by the men of Jabesh-gilead and burned, lest they be further dishonored.

Chapter Eighteen

On the Way to Jerusalem

Place: Near Beth Shan, Galilee Date: Sunday 3 Nisan AD 30

Jesus and the apostles moved toward the Jordan River, they would join with the pilgrims coming from Galilee on the way to Passover in Jerusalem. Probably by pre-arrangement, they joined family and friends from Capernaum, Nazareth, and some of the other Galilean villages.

The little band of apostles led by Jesus began the last journey to Jerusalem. This trip, although unknown to them today, would live long in the minds of those traveling with Jesus. They would be able for years to come to trace each footprint and each event along the way.

They traveled southeast along the border that separated Galilee in the north and Samaria to the south. They were headed for the well-worn path on the east side of Jordan that leads south to Jerusalem. Already pilgrims were on the path, walking in groups, chattering, and occasionally breaking out in song. The trip was always a joyful time, with fellowship along the way and a time of worship at the great temple.

Jesus would share this last trip with those who meant so very much to Him. It was as much a part of His memories as it would be of theirs in the following years.

Ten Lepers Healed

Place: Somewhere Near the Border of Galilee and Samaria

Date: Sunday 3 Nisan AD 30 Reference: Luke 17:11-19

Arriving at an unnamed village, ten lepers approached Jesus, not coming near but keeping the leper's distance, "afar off". This horrible incurable disease had made them social outcasts that must depend upon the kindness and generosity of others for a morsel of food or a scrap of garment. How did they know Jesus? Had the winds carried His name to them? Had others talked of the Man who could heal the sick, cast out demons, and even raise the dead?

We are not told where they had received the information, but today they would do something with it. They cried out, *"Jesus, Master, have mercy on us."* Here alone was their only hope, their only chance, with nothing to offer they cried out for mercy. I do not know whether they dared hope for grace, but it came that day.

Jesus instructed the ten lepers to go show themselves to the priests. (Before they could return to home, family, and work the priests at Jerusalem must determine if they were actually cured of leprosy.) On the road toward Jerusalem, they suddenly noticed a radical change. White spots were disappearing, corrupt flesh was made clean, and the stench of leprosy was passing. They had experienced the miracle of healing.

One of them, a Samaritan, had returned to express his gratitude for healing. (National identity was not important to those who suffered the curse of leprosy. The disease brought them into the fellowship of the outcast.) Jesus expressed disappointment that the nine Jews had failed to glorify God for their healing.

Northern Pharisees Confront Jesus

Place: A Village Near the Samaritan and Galilee Border

Date: Sunday 3 Nisan AD 30 Reference: Luke 17:20-37

(It was probably the same village as the one the lepers were from)

Pharisees were not limited to Jerusalem and its vicinity. Even little villages like the one where the lepers were healed could boast of their own religious zealots. The Pharisees were offended at the praise Jesus gave to the Samaritan leper. They raised a religious question hoping Jesus would not be able to answer or that He would answer in some way that would discredit Himself. They asked when the kingdom of God would come.

They were looking for a kingdom; instead they would get a Saviour and a church. This passage of Scripture in Luke 17 is very similar to Jesus' great Olivet sermon delivered on the Mount of Olives. Jesus used the opportunity to teach the disciples about the Second Coming. Some of the information of Luke 17:21-37 will be given again in Jesus' sermon on Mount Olivet. (Matthew 24-25)

The Pharisees Set a Trap

Place: Somewhere Near the Border of Perea on the Road to Jerusalem

Somewhere on this trip to Jerusalem, the Pharisees attempted to make Jesus agree with one or the other groups in Jerusalem on the question of divorce. The conservatives, under the leadership of Shammai, held a strict view of divorce. The liberals, under Hillel, believed divorce was lawful for every cause. They did not want a real answer; the attempt was to put Jesus at a disadvantage when He arrived at Jerusalem. If He held the views of Shammai, as many believed He would, He certainly would be no more a friend to Herod Antipas than John the Baptist was, and everyone knew what had happened to John the Baptist. Jesus takes neither view, but interprets the intent of God as seen in Eden. He does recognize the hardness of man's heart and expresses the only Scriptural reason for divorce given until this time.

> "And it came to pass, that when Jesus had finished these sayings, he departed from Galilee, and came into the coasts of Judaea beyond Jordan; And great multitudes followed him; and he healed them there. The Pharisees also came unto him, tempting him, and saying unto him, Is it lawful for a man to put away his wife

for every cause? And he answered and said unto them, Have ye not read, that he which made them at the beginning made them male and female, And said, For this cause shall a man leave father and mother, and shall cleave to his wife: and they twain shall be one flesh? Wherefore they are no more twain, but one flesh. What therefore God hath joined together, let not man put asunder. They say unto him, Why did Moses then command to give a writing of divorcement, and to put her away? He saith unto them, Moses because of the hardness of your hearts suffered you to put away your wives: but from the beginning it was not so. And I say unto you, Whosoever shall put away his wife, except it be for fornication, and shall marry another, committeth adultery: and whoso marrieth her which is put away doth commit adultery. His disciples say unto him, If the case of the man be so with his wife, it is not good to marry. But he said unto them, All men cannot receive this saying, save they to whom it is given. For there are some eunuchs, which were so born from their mother's womb: and there are some eunuchs, which were made eunuchs of men: and there be eunuchs, which have made themselves eunuchs for the kingdom of heaven's sake. He that is able to receive it, let him receive it." Matthew 19:1-12

"And if a woman shall put away her husband, and be married to another, she committeth adultery." Mark 10:12

Parables on Prayer

Place: On the Road North of Perea Date: Monday 4 Nisan AD 30

Jesus emphasizes the importance of prayer in two aspects. Persistence in prayer without getting discouraged. Here Jesus told the story of a certain hard hearted judge, which neither respected God or man, who at first had refused to help a widow beaten down by adversaries. The widow persisted until the Judge relented and granted her request. God is not hard hearted, and does care about His own. He will hear our persistent cry.

The second parable would only enflame the Pharisees more. Two men went into the temple to pray, a Pharisee and a publican.[1] The Pharisee spent his prayer bragging about himself and thanked God that he was not like the publican, who was also there praying with him.

The publican, deeply convicted of his life and ways, could not look up but smote himself on the breast saying, "*God be merciful to me a sinner.*" Jesus said this man went home justified, rather than the other.

Again Jesus challenges the hypocrisy of the Pharisees, who made a big show but held in their heart envy and hatred toward the Son of God.

Bring the Little Children unto Me

Place: Unknown Village Date: Monday 4 Nisan AD 30

Nearing some unknown village, the parents brought their little children that Jesus might touch (bless) them. His disciples rebuked the parents and would have sent them away, supposing that Jesus was too busy to receive children. Jesus must have been disappointed that His disciples so misunderstood His relationship with the family and little children. It would have been a welcome

[1] Publicans were gathers of taxes. It was an occupation where both fraud and cheating were commonly practice. They were considered the lowest of men.

relief to be surrounded by little children before those awful days just ahead in Jerusalem.

A Rich Young Ruler Seeks Eternal Life

Place: Below the Border of Samaria and Galilee Date: Monday 4 Nisan AD 30
Reference: Matthew 19:16-26, Mark 10:17-27 and Luke 18:18-27

This young man was probably from one of the villages in southern Perea near the crossing of the Jordan River. Perhaps, as the crowd of pilgrims on the way to Jerusalem passed through his village, he saw Jesus and recognized him, either by having heard him earlier or by reports given in his village. He came running and knelt before Jesus, asking Him, *"Good Master, what shall I do to inherit eternal life?"* Jesus exposed His love of money, and the young ruler went away sorrowful.

The Road to the Cross

Chapter Nineteen

What Will be our Reward?

Reference: Matthew 19:27-30, Mark 10:28-31 and Luke 18:28-30

Peter asked about the rewards of the disciples. After all, they had left a prosperous fishing business to follow Jesus. Earthly rewards did not seem possible at this time. Jesus assures Peter that He is perfectly capable of caring for His servants and rewarding them amply both now and in the world to come. Jesus tells the parable of the householder hiring laborers at all hours of the day and paying them all a full days labor to illustrate the goodness of God in caring for those who labor for Him.

A Private Talk with His Disciples

Place: The Roadside North of the Crossing at Gilgal Date: Tuesday 5 Nisan AD 30
Reference: Matthew 20:17-19

Stopping to rest beside the road, Jesus calls the twelve apostles apart from the crowd. Here, for the third time, Jesus will tell His disciples of His betrayal to the chief priests, His condemnation, deliverance to the Gentiles, and crucifixion. Jesus also speaks of His resurrection on the third day following the crucifixion. Jesus' description leaves nothing to their imagination. We can only look and wonder why the disciples were surprised at the events in Jerusalem only a week later.

Were the disciples hearing but not wanting to hear, believing but not wanting to believe? The events of the crucifixion would leave them scattered and confused.

> "And Jesus going up to Jerusalem took the twelve disciples apart in the way, and said unto them, Behold, we go up to Jerusalem; and the Son of man shall be betrayed unto the chief priests and unto the scribes, and they shall condemn him to death, And shall deliver him to the Gentiles to mock, and to scourge, and to crucify him: and the third day he shall rise again." Matthew 20:17-19

Salome's Request

Place: Gilgal at the Crossing of the Jordan River Date: Wednesday 6 Nisan AD 30
Reference: Matthew 20:20-28 and Mark 10:35-45

At the crossing of the Jordan, Salome[1] comes up from the group of women to ask a special request from Jesus. Salome's request may have been preceded by a request made by her two sons, James and John. The request was for the two seats of authority in the coming kingdom, one on both the right and left hand of Jesus.

---

[1] Salome was the wife of Zebedee and the sister of Mary, the mother of Jesus.

They did not understand the coming of the Church Age and the evangelization of the world. They thought the kingdom age was about to begin. Even at the ascension they were asking, *"Lord wilt thou at this time restore the kingdom to Israel?"* They were overlooking the command to bear witness locally and throughout the world.

> "But ye shall receive power, after that the Holy Ghost is come upon you: and ye shall be witnesses unto me both in Jerusalem, and in all Judaea, and in Samaria, and unto the uttermost part of the earth." Acts 1:8

Now this request for recognition and power did not set well with the other apostles. They may not have overheard Salome's request, but Mark indicates that they overheard James and John requesting the positions. Despite their willingness to suffer with Him, Jesus said the positions were not His to award.

Sharp contention arose among them. They were filled with indignation and begin to argue among themselves about who would be the greatest. This stupid argument was still going on a week later at the Last Supper.

> "And he saith unto them, Ye shall drink indeed of my cup, and be baptized with the baptism that I am baptized with: but to sit on my right hand, and on my left, is not mine to give, but it shall be given to them for whom it is prepared of my Father. And when the ten heard it, they were moved with indignation against the two brethren." Matthew 20:23-24

Blind Bartimaeus and His Friend

Place: At the Ruins of Old Jericho Date: Wednesday 6 Nisan AD 30

Reference: Matthew 20: 29-34, Mark 10:46-52 and Luke 18:35-43

This morning the pilgrims had crossed over the Jordan River and were walking up the road to the city of palm trees known as Jericho. The remains of Old Testament Jericho was just ahead. It offered a place for peddlers of all sorts to sell their fruits, vegetables, and bread to the weary pilgrims before they reached the city limits of the New Testament Jericho.

It was also a good place for the beggars of the city. There was no program for their relief; they must depend upon the generosity of the people who passed by. Every new wave of pilgrims from the north or east was another opportunity to get enough money for food and necessities.

Jericho is about four miles from the Jordan River. It lay this morning as all mornings, basking in the tropical climate of the Jordan depression. Here the weather was warm and pleasant, tropical fruit and plants flourished and food was usually plentiful. In the distance were the Judean mountains and beyond their peaks some fifteen or so miles away was the city of Jerusalem.

Jesus did not pass unnoticed; in fact, a multitude had assembled and was following Him into the city. As they neared the ruins of old Jericho, a blind beggar was shouting something trying to get above the noise of the crowd. In fact, he made so much noise that the disciples tried to "shush" him. But for all their trying, he only grew louder. What was that he was saying, *"Have mercy on us, O Lord, thou son of David."* Us? Yes, Bartimaeus who was the one crying out, had a blind friend with him. *"Have mercy on us, O Lord, thou son of David."*

The cry attracted the attention of Jesus who paused and asked Bartimaeus, "*What will ye that I do unto you?"* Of course, Jesus knew what he wanted, but Bartimaeus needed to say it. *"That I might receive my sight."* Jesus touched their eyes and they could see. They would certainly join the crowd traveling into Jericho.

Zacchaeus

Place: The Entrance into Jericho — Date: Wednesday 6 Nisan AD 30

Reference: Luke 19:1-10

The pilgrims found a warm welcome in Jericho today. There would be much talk about blind Bartimaeus and his friend receiving their sight. Often the people met the pilgrims with warm greetings and even refreshments. Welcome to Jericho!

Many would spend that night in Jericho and sometimes pilgrims would rest another full day before continuing their journey to Jerusalem. As the crowd pressed into the city, a small chief tax collector wanted to catch a glimpse of Jesus. He had no idea that he would meet or talk with Jesus. He just wanted to catch a glimpse and go home to describe the day to his wife and family. Climbing a sycamore tree (a wild fig tree), Zacchaeus could see over the crowd and be away from the insults and threats of the people, who hated the dishonest publicans. Zacchaeus did not know that this day salvation would come to his house and his life would be changed forever.

Jesus stopped directly under the tree and looked up into the face of Zacchaeus sitting on the limb. Jesus knew all about this man sitting on the limb of the sycamore tree. Jesus commanded Zacchaeus to come down; He had planned to abide with him. This would again be a shock treatment to the Pharisees. How could someone who was suppose to be the Messiah or at the least a prophet go home with a rank sinner like Zacchaeus?

Zacchaeus did something that the Pharisees had forgotten how to do. He repented of his sins and was willing to make restitution. His greed became generosity. Half of his goods would go to the poor. Jesus acknowledged that salvation had come that day to the house [family] of Zacchaeus.

Tonight Jesus would attend the synagogue. Normally synagogues held services on the Sabbath [Saturday] and on Monday and Thursday nights. This was Thursday night and Jesus brought a guest with Him, the newly converted Zacchaeus.

It may have been here at the Jericho synagogue that Jesus preached the sermon and told the parable of the pounds. It teaches the responsibility of the servants of God who are entrusted with His possessions. The servant must give an account for the use of these pounds.[2]

[2] The pound is a minah, which equals about three month's wages.

Chapter Twenty

On the Way to Bethany

Place: Jericho, up the mountain to Bethany, Judea   Date: Friday 8 Nisan AD 30

Today is a bright Friday morning and the pilgrims, after their rest at Jericho, will begin the final leg of the journey up the mountain to Bethany and to Jerusalem beyond. The distance is about fifteen miles all uphill. Near the halfway point with the temple and the city of Jerusalem in view, the pilgrims always stopped and sang Psalm 121. The city of Jerusalem lies on the mountainside some seven or so miles away.

> "I will lift up mine eyes unto the hills, from whence cometh my help. My help cometh from the LORD, which made heaven and earth." Psalm 121:1-2

Later today, Jesus will arrive at the home of Martha, Mary, and Lazarus in Bethany, a suburb of Jerusalem. While Jesus and His disciples had turned toward Bethany, the pilgrims probably continued on to Jerusalem just fifteen furlongs away (1.7 miles). Jesus has arrived just six days before Passover, which will be celebrated on Thursday 14 Nisan, with the supper on Friday Evening.

"He said therefore, A certain nobleman went into a far country to receive for himself a kingdom, and to return. And he called his ten servants, and delivered them ten pounds, and said unto them, Occupy till I come. But his citizens hated him, and sent a message after him, saying, We will not have this man to reign over us. And it came to pass, that when he was returned, having received the kingdom, then he commanded these servants to be called unto him, to whom he had given the money, that he might know how much every man had gained by trading. Then came the first, saying, Lord, thy pound hath gained ten pounds. And he said unto him, Well, thou good servant: because thou hast been faithful in a very little, have thou authority over ten cities. And the second came, saying, Lord, thy pound hath gained five pounds. And he said likewise to him, Be thou also over five cities. And another came, saying, Lord, behold, here is thy pound, which I have kept laid up in a napkin: For I feared thee, because thou art an austere man: thou takest up that thou layedst not down, and reapest that thou didst not sow. And he saith unto him, Out of thine own mouth will I judge thee, thou wicked servant. Thou knewest that I was an austere man, taking up that I laid not down, and reaping that I did not sow: Wherefore then gavest not thou my money into the bank, that at my coming I might have required mine own with usury? And he said unto them that stood by, Take from him the pound, and give it to him that hath ten pounds. (And they said unto him, Lord, he hath ten pounds.) For I say unto you, That unto every one which hath shall be given; and from him that hath not, even that he hath shall be taken away from him. But those mine enemies, which would not that I should reign over them, bring hither, and slay them before me." Luke 19:12-27

Chapter Twenty-One

The Anointing at Simon's House

Place: Bethany. Judea - Simon the Leper's Home Date: Saturday 9 Nisan AD 30

The Sabbath began at sundown Friday evening and continued through the daylight hours of Saturday. It was a quiet Sabbath; Jesus probably attended the synagogue at Bethany along with the family of Lazarus. No incident is reported.

The Sabbath ended at sunset, and Simon the leper had planned an evening meal. Meals were often planned to follow on Saturday evening. We know little and much about this Simon of Bethany. For example, we know that he had been a leper and had been healed, and that he had a house in Bethany. We know that he was well to do financially and was a friend of the family of Martha, Mary, and Lazarus. Such a good friend that she was asked to be the hostess at the supper to which Jesus was called.

This meal was no small gathering; Jesus and His disciples were present. Two recent miracles sat at the table - Simon himself, still known as the leper, and Lazarus, who had been raised from the dead after four days in the tomb. Many feel that Matthew and Mark made the supper either Tuesday or Wednesday evening; however, I believe that it occurred on Saturday night before Palm Sunday.

The guests were reclined on their left side and ate with their right hand. Jesus was so inclined during the supper, giving Mary, sister of Martha and Lazarus, an opportunity to anointed Jesus with her treasure, a pound of costly spikenard[1] valued at 300 denarii (this would be the annual wage of a worker). Approaching the table she broke the neck of the bottle and poured the spikenard on His head and His feet.

Judas Iscariot was absolutely furious, *"Why was not this ointment sold for three hundred pence, and given to the poor?"* John explains Judas' concern about the ointment in the following way...

> "This he said, not that he cared for the poor; but because he was a thief, and had the bag, and bare what was put therein." John 12:6

Matthew indicates that Judas initiated the betrayal of Christ. He contacted the priests and settled on a price. From that point on, Judas sought an opportunity to betray Jesus to the high priests. The priests wished to make an arrest without incident and have Jesus killed and out of the way before the multitudes knew what was going on.

---

[1] This was a very expensive ointment that was used as a kind of perfume. It was in a sealed bottle made of alabaster stone.

"Then one of the twelve, called Judas Iscariot, went unto the chief priests, And said unto them, What will ye give me, and I will deliver him unto you? And they covenanted with him for thirty pieces of silver. And from that time he sought opportunity to betray him." Matthew 26:14-16

The Road to the Cross

Chapter Twenty-Two

Palm Sunday

Place: Jerusalem, The Eastern Gate Date: Sunday Morning 10 Nisan AD 30

Just outside the village limits of Bethany, the road to the eastern gate of Jerusalem forks. The right hand fork leads through the village of Bethphage and rejoins the main road near Gethesame, a short distance from the temple gate.

This Sunday morning they left Bethany on their way to the great temple. They would arrive before the morning sacrifice and the hour of prayer at the third hour.[1]

As they neared the fork in the road Jesus asked two of His disciples, probably Peter and John, to go to Bethphage where they would find a donkey and her colt tied. "Untie them and bring them to me. If any man asks you what you are doing just tell them that

[1] The hours begin their numbering with six in the morning, thus the third hour is nine AM, the sixth hour is noon, and the ninth hour is three PM.

the Lord has need of it and he will send it to me. I will send it straightway back to him."

It was only minutes before Peter and John had returned and sure enough they had the two donkeys with them. The colt had never been ridden, the disciples spread their cloaks on its back and Jesus mounted the donkey and started down the hillside into the city of Jerusalem. Today Jesus would fulfill the prophecy of Zechariah.

> "Rejoice greatly, O daughter of Zion; shout, O daughter of Jerusalem: behold, thy King cometh unto thee: he is just, and having salvation; lowly, and riding upon an ass, and upon a colt the foal of an ass." Zechariah 9:9

A large crowd of pilgrims from Galilee had joined the gathering people of Judea in preparation to celebrate the coming Passover. When the news reached the multitude that Jesus was coming to Jerusalem, a great crowd came out to meet Him. Spreading their garments in His path and waving palm branches, they shouted...

> "Hosanna to the son of David: Blessed is he that cometh in the name of the Lord; Hosanna in the highest." Matthew 21:9b

Jesus visits the temple and finds the moneychangers and sellers of sacrifices and trinkets. It was a lucrative business, but more than that it was making merchandise of the House of God. Prices were absorbent and merchants were quick to let you know that their sacrifices and merchandise had both the blessing and the approval of the priests.

Jesus and the apostles leave the city returning to Bethany where they will spend the night with their good friends Martha, Mary, and Lazarus.

Chapter Twenty-Three

Returning to the City of Jerusalem

Place: On the Road to Jerusalem Date: Monday 11 Nisan AD 30

Time: Early Morning Reference: Matthew 21:17-22, Mark 11:12-14 & 20-21

It is early morning; the people are waking, eating breakfast, and getting ready for another busy day in Jerusalem. Jesus has left early for the city and did not join in breakfast. A solitary fig tree grew along the roadway. The figs from this tree were for anyone who picked them. The tree promised much and delivered nothing. Jesus made it an object lesson to the disciples, although Mark suggested it wasn't yet the time for figs.[1]

The fig tree is a type of the nation of Israel and Jesus, who given the opportunity had failed to bring forth fruit for God. Jesus placed a curse on the tree and presently the fig tree withered away.

[1] The fig tree fruit normally appears in Shebat and the green leaves form later in spring. There should have been fruit on the tree.

Jesus' Second Lament over Jerusalem

Place: Headed Down the Mount of Olives Toward the Eastern Gate

Reference: Luke 19:41-42

From the days of David, Jerusalem had been the place to be. God had set His glory in the city and the great Temple of Solomon was its main attraction. When the first temple was lost in 586 BC the captives in far off Babylon sang...

> "How shall we sing the Lord's song in a strange land? If I forget thee, O Jerusalem, let my right hand forget her cunning. If I do not remember thee, let my tongue cleave to the roof of my mouth; if I prefer not Jerusalem above my chief joy." Psalm 137:4-6

They had returned to the land of Judah and many had returned to the city of Jerusalem seventy years later. Zerubbabel, the appointed governor, and Joshua, the high priest, had led the people to finish the second temple in 516 BC, thanks to the encouragement of the prophets Haggai and Zechariah.

When Herod became king in 40 BC through the auspices of his friend Mark Antony, he made every attempt to make the Jews accept him, for he was an Idumean (Edomite). One of the projects of Herod was a renovation and expansion of the temple and the temple area. This project lasted for some forty-six years. Large column porches and an expanded and beautified appearance had been his contribution. But in reality, it was the God of the temple and not the temple itself that mattered most.

This morning Jesus stopped on the road that went down into the Kidron Valley and up again to the eastern gate. With the temple clearly in His view and the city beyond, Jesus, for the second time, laments the destruction of Jerusalem that will come in AD 70 at the hands of the Roman war machine.

Jesus weeps again over the city of Jerusalem and its coming destruction.

> "Saying, If thou hadst known, even thou, at least in this thy day, the things which belong unto thy peace! but now they are hid from thine eyes. For the days shall come upon thee, that thine enemies shall cast a trench about thee, and compass thee round, and keep thee in on every side, And shall lay thee even with the ground, and thy children within thee; and they shall not leave in thee one stone upon another; because thou knewest not the time of thy visitation." Luke 19:42-44

Cleansing the Temple for the Last Time

Place: Jerusalem - The Temple　　　　Date: Monday 11 Nisan AD 30

Caiaphas and Annas had a lucrative trade system in the temple. Money must be exchanged, and a moneychanger ran their tables and charged an absorbent handling fee. Approved sacrificial animals were for sale within the gentile section of the temple, each at several times its true value. Annas and Caiaphas received a healthy portion of each transaction made within the temple.

Entering Jerusalem, Jesus makes His way to the temple. Three years ago, He had, with a scourge made of cords, drove out the crooked money changers and the commercializers that were taking advantage of the pilgrims coming to worship.

Last Sunday He watched their thieving tactics and this morning it was too much to bear. Jesus was very angry and once more He would clean the House of God. Jesus turned over their booths and tables and drove them out of the temple area. He proclaimed that His Father's house was to be a **house of prayer**, but these men had made it a den of thieves.

Two Small Coins

Place: Jerusalem - The Temple   Date: Monday 11 Nisan AD 30

While in the temple, Jesus watched the people give. Near the entrance/exit of the temple stood two large containers shaped like trumpets. As worshippers came and went, they dropped their offering into these containers. Many rich people had cast in much, and well they should, but a poor widow gave all she had, just two mites. Jesus commended her giving to the disciples.

Outside the temple area, some Greeks were trying to see Jesus. They came to Philip, he was the only disciple with a Greek name, and asked to see Jesus. Philip was uncertain what to do with these foreigners. Finding Andrew, who always seemed to know what to do, they brought the delegation to Jesus.

Chapter Twenty-Four

Final Attempts to Find a Charge Against Jesus

Place: Jerusalem - The Temple Porches

Date: Late Afternoon Monday 11 Nisan or Early Tuesday Morning 12 Nisan AD 30

The First Trap

Place: On the Temple Porch with many Spectators

Reference: Matthew 22:15 - 21

Desperately the Jews needed some political charge against Jesus. The Romans were not likely to act on the religious mumble jumble that they were trying to concoct against Jesus. In their quest, the Pharisees sought the aid of an unpopular political party, at least, they were unpopular with the general public; however, they did have great political clout with the Romans.

Ringed about by the Pharisees and the people, the Herodians[1] bring up a very controversial subject. *"Is it lawful to give tribute to Caesar or not?"* They had Him now; at least they thought they had Him. If He answered no, then they had a valid indictment to present to the Roman governor, Pilate. His answer would be considered an act of sedition. If Jesus' answer indicated that the taxation was appropriate, the Jews, who hated the taxation, the publicans, and the Roman occupation of Israel, would be angry. He would surely say the wrong thing one way or another.

They had the wrong man this time, for He knew their hearts and perceived their wickedness. Jesus requested a coin and someone handed Him a denarii, a silver coin equal to a days work. One side of the coin had a picture of Caesar on it. "Whose image and superscription is this?" Jesus asked. They replied, *"Caesar's."* Jesus, still holding the coin, calmly said...

> "Render therefore unto Caesar the things which are Caesar's; and unto God the things that are God's." Matthew 22:21

---

[1] The Herodians were Jews that supported the ruling family of the Herods. They were more political than religious; however, they did hold to the Jewish faith but were very liberal. They would have been better accepted in the company of the Sadducees than the Pharisees.

The Second Trap

Place: Jesus was still in the Temple Date: Same Day Monday 11 Nisan AD 30

The Sadducees were led by the high priest Caiaphas[2] and his father-in-law Annas.[3] They, along with all the other high priests,[4] were all of the sect of the Sadducees. These were non-Bible believers in high religious positions. It is still practiced to this very day. Pastors and spiritual leaders who deny the inspiration and infallibility of the Bible occupy pulpits and chairs in colleges or universities from which they denounce the truth in the name of truth and are liars.

These spiritual leaders did not seem to care that their faulty belief was far from the more orthodox views of the people. They denied the Scriptures, accepting only parts of the Pentateuch and nothing else. They denied life after death, the physical bodily resurrection, the judgments of God, angels, and heaven and hell. There was nothing orthodox about these boys, and their ungodly influence had

---

[2] Caiaphas had become high priest following his father-in-law, Annas. He had come into the office in AD 18 and was removed in AD 37 by the Roman procurator [governor]. His name will appear in the trial of Jesus and in the early years of the Church. The family of Annas, which he had married into, was very rich and their prestige and education gave them a superior standing. The ruling priests were usually family members. All were of the sect of the Sadducees.

[3] Annas was the father-in-law of Caiaphas. He had been high priest in AD 6-15 and had been removed from office by the Roman procurator. However, this old man formed a dynasty of high priests using his sons and his son-in-law. While Caiaphas speaks officially, rest assuredly that Annas still ran the priesthood.

[4] There was only one high priest; however, many held high positions in the priesthood and so they are often mentioned as high priests.

filtered down the priesthood until most of the priests agreed with them or did not dare disagree with them.

To these liberals the body resurrection of the dead was utter nonsense and today they would show just how illiterate the Rabbi Jesus really was. If they could back Him down on their hypothetical question, they might show the people that He was not the champion of their cause, for most of them believed in the resurrection.

The hypothetical question concerned seven brothers who had married the same woman, one after another until all were dead. The were referring to the law of levirate,[5] where the closest kinsman marries the widow in order to raise up heirs to the dead husband and to redeem any property that belonged to the family.

One by one the husbands had died and she had been the wife of them all. Now they asked, "*Whose wife will she be in the resurrection?*"

Jesus knew the problem of these men was not the resurrection, but a total lack of spiritual knowledge, for they had rejected the very Word of God. So He said...

> "Jesus answered and said unto them, Ye do err, not knowing the scriptures, nor the power of God. For in the resurrection they neither marry, nor are given in marriage, but are as the angels of

[5] Boaz and Ruth from the Old Testament are an excellent example of the levirate marriage.

> God in heaven.[6] But as touching the resurrection of the dead, have ye not read that which was spoken unto you by God, saying, I am the God of Abraham, and the God of Isaac, and the God of Jacob? God is not the God of the dead, but of the living. And when the multitude heard this, they were astonished at his doctrine." Matthew 22:29-33

The Third Trap

Reference: Matthew 22:34-40 and Mark 12:28-34

The Sadducees had blown it, and the Pharisees knew they would. Now it was up to them, if Jesus was to be discredited in the eyes of the people. They held a strategy meeting, and one of them, who was also a scribe, decided to ask Jesus what was the greatest commandment. All had their favorite commandment, but it seemed that the favorite of all the Pharisees must have been commandment number four, for they harped on it more than all the others.

Jesus simply quoted from Deuteronomy 6:5 and Leviticus 19:18 by saying...

> "Jesus said unto him, Thou shalt love the Lord thy God with all thy heart, and with all thy soul, and with all thy mind. This is the first and great commandment. And the second is like unto it, Thou shalt love thy neighbour as thyself. On these two commandments hang all the law and the prophets." Matthew 22:37-40

---

[6] Some have interpreted this verse to mean that the angels are without gender, neither male nor female. This is absolutely not true. Men and women will not lose their gender in the resurrection nor will they lose their companionship.

The scribe admitted that Jesus had the correct answer, even including the statement on loving thy neighbor. Jesus said to him...

> "Thou art not far from the kingdom of God." Mark 12:34b

These questions and the open attack on Jesus brought forth the strongest denouncement of the Pharisees found in the Bible. Jesus pronounces seven woes on them in Matthew 23.

The Road to the Cross

Chapter Twenty-Five

The Sermon on the Mount of Olives

Place: Jerusalem - On Mt Olivet   Date: Early Morning Tuesday 12 Nisan AD 30

This morning, as they left Bethany going to Jerusalem, they passed by where the fig tree was that Jesus cursed. It was withered and dried up at the roots.

Jesus and the disciples visited the temple this morning and Judas slipped away from the group to finalize his agreement to betray Jesus to the chief priest. A multitude of Galileans and pilgrims from everywhere were in town, so the arrest of Jesus must be made in secret and the trial and execution must be done speedily. They would need Judas to give them a secluded place to make the arrest, preferably at night.

Luke gave this explanation for such a vile deed of Judas...

> "Then entered Satan into Judas surnamed Iscariot, being of the number of the twelve. And he went his way, and communed with the chief priests and captains, how he might betray him unto them. And they were glad, and covenanted to give him money. And he promised, and sought opportunity to betray him unto them in the absence of the multitude." Luke 22:3-6

The Temple Building

Perhaps forgetting who he was, Jesus' disciples were showing Him the great structure of the temple. The great stones and buildings very impressive. Jesus said...

> "verily I say unto you, There shall not be one stone left upon another, that shall not be thrown down." Matthew 24:2b

Jesus' Sermon on Eschatology

The disciples were interested in eschatology; they asked Jesus three questions.

1. When shall these things be?
2. What shall be the sign of thy coming?
3. What shall be the sign of the end of the world?

This is called the Olivet Discourse. In His sermon, Jesus describes the coming Tribulation and a brief description of the rapture and the revelation when He comes at the end of the Tribulation. You will find much of what is said in Revelation in an abbreviated form.

Two parables will conclude the sermon, the parable of the ten virgins and the parable of the talents. Both are understood only in the light of Jesus' return for His Church. In the sermon, Jesus reveals the Judgment of Living Nations that will occur at the end of the tribulation. This is the only place this judgment is mentioned or explained.

> "When the Son of man shall come in his glory, and all the holy angels with him, then shall he sit upon the throne of his glory: And before him shall be gathered all nations: and he shall separate them one from another, as a shepherd divideth his sheep from the goats: And he shall set the sheep on his right hand, but the goats on the left. Then shall the King say unto them on his right hand, Come, ye blessed of my Father, inherit the kingdom prepared for you from the foundation of the world:" Matthew 25:31-34

Jesus also gives the end of Satan and his angels in chapter twenty-five.

> "Then shall he say also unto them on the left hand, Depart from me, ye cursed, into everlasting fire, prepared for the devil and his angels:" Matthew 25:41

Chapter Twenty-Six

The Last Passover in Jerusalem

Place: Jerusalem Date: Tuesday Morning 12 Nisan AD 30

Jesus had just spent His last night in the home of His dear friends at Bethany; He would not return. Tonight, He would face the great ordeal of His mission. The sun was bright and the journey pleasant covering the two miles into Jerusalem. It was just two days until Passover. The Passover meal would be on Friday night after 6:00 PM on the Jewish day of 15 Nisan.

On the road to Jerusalem, they passed the fig tree. It was full of leaves yesterday, but because it produced no fruit, Jesus placed a curse on it. Today it was dried up from the roots.

Peter and John are sent ahead of the main group. Their duty was to locate the place for the Passover meal and make all necessary preparations. Peter and John were the natural selections, Peter for his leadership and John because he was well acquainted with the city.

The exact place of the meal is kept secret from the group. Jesus did not want Judas, who was seeking an opportunity to betray Him, to know where the meal would take place. The disciples are told to watch for a man bearing a water pitcher and to follow him. Jesus said the owner would provide a large upper room suitable for the occasion and she did. The huge home belonged to Mary, the mother of John Mark and sister to Barnabas. This upper room would become a favorite meeting place for weeks to come.

Who Will Wash Feet?

Place: Jerusalem – The Upper Room in Mary's House
Date: Wednesday Night 13 Nisan AD 30

This afternoon, Jesus and the disciples visited the public bathhouse somewhere in Jerusalem. Making their way through the narrow winding streets, they reached Mary's house and the upper room as the evening shadows grew deep. It was customary for either a servant or one of the group to wash the feet of those coming in from the dirty streets. The guest would remove their sandals, dip their feet in a basin, and the servant would dry them. They would take their meal with bare feet.

None of the disciples offered to wash feet, that is the duty of a servant. The offense of the request of James, John, and Salome still rang in their ears. Who was the greatest among them? Each was carrying a load of his own importance. Who was the greatest among them? Did it really matter? As the meal ended, Jesus taught them a lesson they would never forget. Jesus, rising from the table, picked up the towel and basin and began to wash the feet of all the disciples. They protruded over the end of the couch where they were laying. What a lesson in humility! And what a spiritual lesson on the necessity of daily cleansing in order to maintain our fellowship with Him.

During the Meal

The meal was eaten reclined on the left side using the right hand for eating. Judas Iscariot was on Jesus' left and John was on His right. Directly across the table form John was Peter, the other disciples were scattered around the table.

As the meal began, Jesus announced that one of the disciples would betray Him. It went around the table like wildfire. On every lip was the question, *"Is it I?"* Jesus did not answer the question. But Peter must have an answer, always imperative, always inquisitive, he needed to know. Peter signaled John across the table to ask Jesus who it was. Peter did not expect Jesus to say it before the group; but figured that He would tell John and he could find out later. Apparently Jesus told John, who was laying on His right side, but in tones not loud enough for anyone else to hear. That night, when Judas left the room, three people knew where he was going, Jesus, Judas, and John.

Sometime during the meal, Jesus took the unleavened Passover bread, blessed and brake it, and gave it to the disciples and said...

> "This is my body which is given for you: this do in remembrance of me." Luke 22:19b

Taking the Passover cup, Jesus blessed it and said...

> "This cup is the new testament in my blood, which is shed for you." Luke 22:20b

Jesus institutes an ordnance of remembrance. It was to be practiced by His disciples until His return for them. The emblems were not flesh or blood, but bread and grape juice; they were used as symbols and nothing more. The purpose is clearly stated, *"This do in remembrance of Me"*, and in doing it we do show His death until He returns.

The Betrayal

Quietly Judas slips into the night, Jesus' last bit of advice to Judas was *"That thou doest, do quickly."* Judas hopes to bring the priest and temple police to this quiet upper room to arrest Jesus. However, Jesus still had other things to do before the arrest.

The Sermon in the Upper Room

Still seated at the table, Jesus began one of three great sermons. The other two were probably preached on the way to the Kedron Valley and the garden at the Mount of Olives.

Knowing the fear and panic that would come to the disciples, Jesus said...

> "Let not your heart be troubled: ye believe in God, believe also in me. In my Father's house are many mansions: if it were not so, I would have told you. I go to prepare a place for you. And if I go and prepare a place for you, I will come again, and receive you unto myself; that where I am, there ye may be also. And whither I go ye know, and the way ye know. Thomas saith unto him, Lord, we know not whither thou goest; and how can we know the way? Jesus saith unto him, I am the way, the truth, and the life: no man cometh unto the Father, but by me." John 14:1-6

Great comfort was offered concerning the coming of the Holy Spirit, which Jesus referred to as the Comforter.[1]

The Comforter was to be permanent. He would abide forever. No conditions were given for this permanent arrangement. John has featured Jesus comments on the security of those who believe in Him. They have eternal life, they shall never perish, and they cannot be plucked from the hand of God. Now this is an exciting verse of promise, Jesus will send someone to help us and under no condition will He ever leave us.

> "And I will pray the Father, and he shall give you another Comforter, that he may abide with you for ever," John 14:16

The Comforter, who is the Holy Ghost, will recall all things to the mind of the apostles. It will be through the Holy Spirit that they will formulate the Apostles Doctrine, the New Testament.

Jesus and the disciples quietly left the upper room coming down the stairs at the side of the house and headed for the Garden of

[1] The Greek word is Paraclete and means *one who comes along side of us to strengthen and help.*

Gethesame. There was work to be done there and Jesus would not wish to bring harm to Mary or her house. Just before they left, they sang the Hallel, a group of the Psalms beginning with Psalm 113.

> "Praise ye the LORD. Praise, O ye servants of the LORD, praise the name of the LORD. Blessed be the name of the LORD from this time forth and for evermore. From the rising of the sun unto the going down of the same the Lord's name is to be praised. The LORD is high above all nations, and his glory above the heavens. Who is like unto the LORD our God, who dwelleth on high, Who humbleth himself to behold the things that are in heaven, and in the earth! He raiseth up the poor out of the dust, and lifteth the needy out of the dunghill; That he may set him with princes, even with the princes of his people. He maketh the barren woman to keep house, and to be a joyful mother of children. Praise ye the LORD." Psalm 113:1-9

It closes with Psalm 118 (I have included only the first six verses of Psalm 118).

> "O give thanks unto the LORD; for he is good: because his mercy endureth for ever. Let Israel now say, that his mercy endureth for ever. Let the house of Aaron now say, that his mercy endureth for ever. Let them now that fear the LORD say, that his mercy endureth for ever. I called upon the LORD in distress: the LORD answered me, and set me in a large place. The LORD is on my side; I will not fear: what can man do unto me?" Psalm 118:1-6

Sermon on the Vine

Place: On the way to Gethsemane

Jesus continued the message or started another one after they left the upper room. The sermon is highlighted in this passage.

> "I am the vine, ye are the branches: He that abideth in me, and I in him, the same bringeth forth much fruit: for without me ye can do nothing." John 15:5

The Final Sermon

Place: In the Kedron Valley Near the Garden at the Base of the Mount of Olives

Date: Wednesday 13 Nisan AD 30

The final sermon is recorded in John 16. It finished His message on the Holy Spirit. The sermon may be characterized by this explanation that Jesus gave His disciples.

> "Nevertheless I tell you the truth; It is expedient for you that I go away: for if I go not away, the Comforter will not come unto you; but if I depart, I will send him unto you." John 16:7

Chapter Twenty-Seven

In the Garden

Place: Gethesame in the Kedron Valley | Time: About 8:00 PM

In the shadows of the garden, the disciples paused to rest. Jesus, taking Peter, James, and John, went deeper into the garden and begins the great high priestly prayer of John 17. Three times He would return and find the disciples asleep. He was disappointed in their watch, but nevertheless, there were few words of condemnation spoken by Jesus.

Sometime during the in the garden hours, God laid on Jesus the sins of every person who would ever by faith receive Him as their Saviour. The synoptic Gospels give a very short prayer of Jesus, but Doctor Luke does take a serious look at our sin-bearer and said...

> "And there appeared an angel unto him from heaven, strengthening him. And being in an agony he prayed more earnestly: **and his sweat was as it were great drops of blood falling down to the ground."** Luke 22:43-44

When Jesus appeared before the high priest, He was already bearing your sins in His own body.

> "For he hath made him to be sin for us, who knew no sin; that we might be made the righteousness of God in him." II Corinthians 5:21

> "Who his own self bare our sins in his own body on the tree, that we, being dead to sins, should live unto righteousness: by whose stripes ye were healed." I Peter 2:24

As He left the garden that evening, Jesus was carrying all the wicked things that we would ever do. God, in His foreknowledge, looked down through the ages and saw those who would believe, saw their individual sins and needs, and laid them all on Jesus.

The Arrest

There was the sound of men coming through the darkness. They were carrying torches and were armed. People came and went from the garden at night, but this was a mob not a group of men seeking a place to rest.

Jesus knew who they were, but He stepped to the front and said, *"Who seek ye?"* Judas stepped out of the group and kissed Jesus, and Jesus said unto him, *"Judas, betrayest thou the Son of man with a kiss?"* Then Jesus announced Himself. Suddenly the mob went backward and fell to the ground.

Peter ever a man of action, drew his sword and went to the attack. He struck at the man closest to him; hitting his helmet and coming down, he sliced off his right ear. Malchus was glad for a good helmet for Peter was no ear slicer. The sword must have hit the helmet and came down its side to clip off the man's ear. Peter was ready to fight for Jesus no matter how big the mob. These were not Roman soldiers, but the temple priests, police, and servants. Peter had sworn his allegiance to Jesus at the Last Supper.

> "And he said unto him, Lord, I am ready to go with thee, both into prison, and to death." Luke 22:33

But Jesus had warned him that before daylight, he would deny Him three times.

> "And he said, I tell thee, Peter, the cock shall not crow this day, before that thou shalt thrice deny that thou knowest me." Luke 22:34

Now he would prove that allegiance and a man's ear lay on the ground as evidence. But Jesus stopped Peter and picking up the ear from the ground, Jesus reattached it. Luke is the only Gospel writer that tells us about this ear reattachment. As a physician, it would certainly get and hold his attention. No one had ever seen anything just like that. John tells us that the name of the man was Malchus and that he was a servant of the high priest. Having stopped Peter, Jesus said...

> "Then said Jesus unto him, Put up again thy sword into his place: for all they that take the sword shall perish with the sword. Thinkest thou that I cannot now pray to my Father, and he shall

> presently give me more than twelve legions of angels?" Matthew 26:52-53

This was more than seventy-two thousand angels. If one angel could take care of one hundred and eighty-five thousand Assyrians in one night, just think what twelve legions of angels could have done with this meager group.

Jesus asked the mob of temple police, priests, and servants a very pertinent question, John said that He asked basically the same question to Caiaphas.

> "Then Jesus said unto the chief priests, and captains of the temple, and the elders, which were come to him, Be ye come out, as against a thief, with swords and staves? When I was daily with you in the temple, ye stretched forth no hands against me: but this is your hour, and the power of darkness." Luke 22:52-53

Binding Jesus, they led Him away to Annas' house, who was father-in-law to Caiaphas, the high priest. John went with Him, and Peter followed afar off. The rest of the disciples were scattered into the night.

> "Then the band and the captain and officers of the Jews took Jesus, and bound him, And led him away to Annas first; for he was father in law to Caiaphas, which was the high priest that same year. Now Caiaphas was he, which gave counsel to the Jews, that it was expedient that one man should die for the people. And Simon Peter followed Jesus, and so did another disciple: that disciple was known unto the high priest, and went in with Jesus into the palace of the high priest." John 18:12-15

> "Then took they him, and led him, and brought him into the high priest's house. And Peter followed afar off." Luke 22:54

The Garden Streaker

Only Mark tells us about this incident in the garden. There was a young man there wrapped only in a linen cloth, probably a bed sheet, and when someone tried to arrest him, they grabbed the sheet and the young man fled the garden naked. Who was he?

We aren't told, but I believe there is ample evidence to point to young John Mark, probably only a teenager. He had been awaken when the mob, led by Judas, came to his house seeking Jesus. Fearing for the safety of the group, young Mark jump up, pulled a sheet from his bed, wrapped it around him, and went running out the back way to warn Jesus and the disciples in the garden. He was still there when the mob arrived. Someone spotted him and believed he would be a good catch, being the only son of the wealthy mother, Mary, of Jerusalem. Leaving the sheet in the grasp of one of the mob, Mark fled in the darkness toward home.

Chapter Twenty-Eight

The Religious Trials - The Palace of Annas

Place: Jerusalem - Annas, the Former High Priest's Palace

Date: Wednesday Night 13 Nisan AD 30

Annas may not have been the high priest, but it was certain that he was the power in Jerusalem. He had been high priest but had been removed by the Roman Procurator, and even then he had been successful in getting Caiaphas appointed. A preliminary hearing was held and they sought to finalize some charge against Jesus with witnesses.

John, who was known to the high priest and his servants, had no problem getting into the hearing; however, Peter was not permitted entry until John spoke to the girl who kept the main gate that entered out into the city street beyond. When she admitted Peter she asked him, *"Art thou not one of this man's disciples?"* Peter without thinking replied immediately, *"I am not."* Once inside, Peter joined the group at the center pavilion fire. At the fire, one said unto Peter, *"Art thou one of his disciples?"* Again, Peter denied knowing Jesus. A cock must have crowed; it was probably 3 AM. Later a group found Peter by the porch; they accused him of being a Galilean and one of Jesus disciples. With an oath Peter denied that he even knew Jesus. Again he had denied him, this time he denied being one of the disciples of Jesus, and the cock crowed the second time. Moreover, Luke tells us that Jesus turned and looked at Peter.

> "And the Lord turned, and looked upon Peter. And Peter remembered the word of the Lord, how he had said unto him, Before the cock crow, thou shalt deny me thrice. And Peter went out, and wept bitterly." Luke 22:61-62

Before Caiaphas

Place: Jerusalem - At the Palace of the High Priest Caiaphas

Date: 13 Nisan AD 30 Time: 10 PM until 3 AM

Annas apparently had tried to get the charge against Jesus defined and proved, and had failed. So Jesus is sent bound into the more formal chambers of the high priest Caiaphas. It was probably just next door for Annas and Caiaphas shared the same courtyard. Other members of the prestigious Sanhedrin Court had been called to the hearing. They had all agreed that they must kill Jesus and now they are called in to formally condemn Jesus to death.

Everything about the trial was illegal, no trial was held after dark and before only a few men, and the charge was absolutely ridiculous. They said...

> "This fellow said, I am able to destroy the temple of God, and build it in three days." Matthew 26:61b

Even so, the witnesses could not agree. Were they afraid that Jesus and His followers would make an assault on the temple and raise the ire of the Romans?

Finally, pressed for some religious statement to bring a hearing before the Sanhedrin, Caiaphas seeks some sort of confession from Jesus.

> "And the high priest arose, and said unto him, Answerest thou nothing? what is it which these witness against thee? But Jesus held his peace. And the high priest answered and said unto him, I adjure thee by the living God, that thou tell us whether thou be the Christ, the Son of God. Jesus saith unto him, Thou hast said: nevertheless I say unto you, Hereafter shall ye see the Son of man sitting on the right hand of power, and coming in the clouds of heaven. Then the high priest rent his clothes, saying, He hath spoken blasphemy; what further need have we of witnesses? behold, now ye have heard his blasphemy. What think ye? They answered and said, He is guilty of death. Then did they spit in his face, and buffeted him; and others smote him with the palms of their hands, Saying, Prophesy unto us, thou Christ, Who is he that smote thee?" Matthew 26:62-68

The last hours of the night passed with the servants and temple police abusing Jesus. They mocked and smote Him, and then they played the childish game of guess who. They blindfolded Jesus then struck Him and asked Him to identify the striker. My dear friend, a blindfold on the eyes of God means nothing. Every sin is open before Him and none struck Him without His full knowledge. If only they knew, He knew their name, their life, and their future.

Blasphemous words fell from their hardened lips, no doubt by the false statements of the priests and Pharisees.

During the early morning hours, messengers were very busy assembling the members of the Sanhedrin Court. The court met in one of the rooms of the temple. Of course, they did not want every member of the court, just those who were in full agreement with them. There were members whom they knew were sympathetic to Jesus and His disciples.

With selected members they could get a unanimous decision of the court. This would be helpful when they approached Pilate. It was rumored, and they believed it to be true, that some members of the court were sympathetic to Christ and His disciples, and others, especially Nicodemus and Joseph of Arimathaea, were reported as being His followers. They might come, but no one would send after them. They would select only those whom they knew were in full agreement with them, believing that the death of Jesus was important in order to save the nation.

Before the Sanhedrin Court

Place: Jerusalem - The Sanhedrin Court Room in the Temple

Date: Wednesday 13 Nisan AD 30 Time: 5 AM to 6 AM

The light of dawn had just begin drifting down the streets of Jerusalem as the chief priest escorted by the temple guards moved Jesus to the official judgment hall of the Sanhedrin. The room was dark and chilly, soon oil lamps were flickering, driving the darkness into the remote corners of the room.

It was too early, they all knew that the court never met at this hour, but there were things that must be accomplished today and they must start early to get it done. There were two obvious reasons why they must finish this thing today. First, they did not want a riot on their hands by giving the Galileans time to realize what was happening and secondly, tomorrow was to be a high day, the day of preparation for the Passover.

Caiaphas takes his seat and the court is called to order. It is very oblivious that all seventy judges are not present in the courtroom, in fact, it seems that far too many seats were vacant, not even a quorum was present. Never the less, they could handle this business and they would take their chances later.

The trial, after all, was a mere formality; they had already reached the verdict of guilty and pronounced the sentence.

> "And the high priest answered and said unto him, I adjure thee by the living God, that thou tell us whether thou be the Christ, the Son of God. Jesus saith unto him, Thou hast said: nevertheless I say unto you, Hereafter shall ye see the Son of man sitting on the right hand of power, and coming in the clouds of heaven. Then the high priest rent his clothes, saying, He hath spoken blasphemy; what further need have we of witnesses? behold, now ye have heard his blasphemy. What think ye? **They answered and said, He is guilty of death."** Matthew 26:63b-66

The executive council had already reached their verdict and passed the sentence the night before; they needed only to legalize the actions in a formal court meeting. However, a serious problem confronted them. Both Pilate and Herod Antipas were in the city. Addition troops were present for crowd control and any move they made without his permission might upset the balance of power.

After all, this was the better way, let the Romans do it and to some degree they could wash their hands of the whole matter. They could get Him crucified with some civil charge against Him and it would seem a little like the Romans fault.

Since they could not execute Jesus, they must trick Pilate into carrying out their death sentence. They believed that Pilate would have little problem executing another Jew, but in case he did, they had political clout. It would be done.

The Road to the Cross

Chapter Twenty-Nine

The Death of the Betrayer

Place: The Temple Area and Beyond the Dung Gate in the Valley of Hinnon

Judas had followed Jesus from the garden, trying to hide himself among the crowd. Things may not have gone as well as he expected. He was close enough to see the miracles of the garden, the falling back of the crowd when Jesus spoke, and then there was the severed ear of Malchus. It had been replaced without a stitch by the hand of Jesus.

Judas had followed through the hearing procedures at the home of Annas and Caiaphas. In the early hours of dawn, he had heard the final verdict and watched them lead Jesus bound to Pilate. Judas was filled with remorse, how could this ever be made right?

Judas went to the temple and into the court of the Jewish men. There he found a few priests; it seemed that some of these were among those with whom he had struck the bargain to betray Christ. The coins were like weights in his bag and their jingle brought back memories in his life. How could he have ever done this? To the priest he said, *"I have sinned in that I have betrayed the innocent blood."* To which the priest replied, *"What is that to us? see thou to that."* (Matthew 27:4) It was very obvious that they considered Judas' guilt his problem and not theirs. They would have no part of receiving the blood money back into the temple treasury.

Judas, standing in the Jewish court was a long way from the door of the temple, but he was now in deep remorse and angry, so with all his strength he threw the silver coins through the door of the great temple and into the quiet sanctuary. Horrified, the priests gathered it up, trying to decide what to do with it. Their decision fulfilled the prophecy of the Scriptures.

> "And I said unto them, If ye think good, give me my price; and if not, forbear. So they weighed for my price thirty pieces of silver. And the LORD said unto me, Cast it unto the potter: a goodly price that I was prised at of them. And I took the thirty pieces of silver, and cast them to the potter in the house of the LORD." Zechariah 11:12-13

Judas' repentance was not genuine. He was sorry that all knew him for a traitor and sorry that he had betrayed innocent blood, but there was no sense of changing direction with his life. Judas left the city through one of the city gates and probably headed for the Hinnon Valley, it was the garbage dump of the city. There, perhaps on the limb of a tree, he tied a cord about his neck and jumped to his death. The only other book that reports Judas' death is Acts and it leaves a gruesome scene in our mind.

"Men and brethren, this scripture must needs have been fulfilled, which the Holy Ghost by the mouth of David spake before concerning Judas, which was guide to them that took Jesus. For he was numbered with us, and had obtained part of this ministry. **Now this man purchased a field with the reward of iniquity; and falling headlong, he burst asunder in the midst, and all his bowels gushed out.** And it was known unto all the dwellers at Jerusalem; insomuch as that field is called in their proper tongue, Aceldama, that is to say, The field of blood." Acts 1:16-19

Chapter Thirty

The Civil Trials - The Man Pontius Pilate

Pontius Pilate had become governor of Judah in 26 AD and ruled until 36 AD, while it may seem like a short reign; however, the four governors before Pilate had only reigned a total of twenty years. Pilate was about the same age as Jesus, somewhere in his early thirties. Pilate was a very proud, obstinate, hot tempered Roman. His wife was Claudia Procula, granddaughter of the Emperor Augustus, she was the illegitimate daughter of Claudia, third wife of the Emperor Tiberius. It was probably through her that Pilate had secured this position that made him ruler over Judea, Samaria, and Edom.

When he arrived in Judea, Pilate discovered that there was no statue to the Roman Emperor in the town square of Jerusalem. In fact, that was the only major city in the Roman Empire where there was no statue of the Emperor. Augustus had promised the Jews that no statues would be erected in Jerusalem. The city had been exempt from Emperor worship, but Pilate was about to change that.

On his very first trip to Jerusalem, the soldiers were carrying images of the Caesar on their standards. Reaching the Roman fortress, Pilate had the standards hung on the wall of the fortress facing down into the temple area.

Pilate well imagined that the Jews would attack the fortress and remove the images, and if they did, he would have a perfect excuse for punishing them severely. However, the cunning Pilate was out smarted by the high priest Caiaphas. He gathered the Jews together adding men as they went and arrived at Caesurae 7000 strong. For a week, they picketed the Procurator's residence, so that each time he came out he heard them praying for his soul. Pilate finally agreed to meet with them in the market place, planning a massacre. The Jews sensing what Pilate had planned knelt down exposing themselves willing rather to die than have images in Jerusalem. Pilate was humiliated and ordered the removal of the images never to try placing images there again.

A second incident came a bit later; Pilate wanted to run an aqueduct into the city bringing fresh water from the south. However, there was not enough funds for the project and Pilate dipped into the temple treasury to finance his project. When a riot broke out, Pilate sent troops dressed in plain clothing with clubs to put it down. Thousands were killed in the panic and a report of this was sent to Rome, Pilate received a severe reprimand from Rome over the incident.

Jesus mentions another incident when Pilate, for some reason unknown to us, killed several Galileans as they were sacrificing, and mixed their blood with the blood of their sacrifices.

> "There were present at that season some that told him of the Galilaeans, whose blood Pilate had mingled with their sacrifices." Luke 13:1

Pilate had not come off very good in his relationship with Caiaphas and Annas. In fact, from the rebukes he had received from Rome, he must have felt that he was on pretty shaky ground in Jerusalem.

On Trial Before Pilate

Place: Jerusalem - The Fortress Antonia Date: Wednesday 13 Nisan AD 30
Time: About 6 AM

The Jewish business day begin with sunrise and already people were moving in the streets. The crowd was not yet large; it was time to move quickly. The room where the Sanhedrin met was in the temple; it would be a small distance to the Fortress Antonia.

However, there was another major problem for them, if they entered the judgment hall in the Fortress Antonia they would be defiled for the coming Passover. Since the high priest and temple officials were key players in the Passover celebration, they had to be very careful of contamination.

Pilate moved his Praetorium to the pavement,[1] a large stone covered area inside the Fortress Antonia. A band of soldiers, ringed the Gabbatha (a cohort of literally 600 soldiers), were assembled in the area. The Praetorium was simple to set up, all Pilate needed do was to move his judgment seat into the area and hang up his official shield and it was now officially the Praetorium.

Pilate had yielded to their demands, his experience with Caiaphas had not been pleasant and he did not want further trouble from Rome. Pilate's question to the group was...

> "What accusation bring ye against this man?" John 18:29b

His question was answered in a defiant manner by the delegation led by Caiaphas and Annas.

> "If he were a malefactor [criminal], we would not have delivered him up unto thee." John 18:30

The charges had been formalized and they looked impressive enough; however, Pilate saw through their scheme. They would use him to rid themselves of someone they viewed as a threat to themselves or their lucrative religious system.

According to Luke 23:2, the high priests brought three charges against Jesus. They were all lies but really that did not matter to these men dead set on killing an innocent man.

---

[1] The "Pavement" or in Hebrew the "Gabbatha" was a stone covered parade ground.

(1) We found this fellow perverting our nation.
(2) He forbid to give tribute to Caesar.
(3) He himself is Christ, a King.

It was this last charge that caught the attention of Pilate, was this another rebel? There certainly had been others before Him. Was this another rebel from the hills of Galilee? Was He any threat to the peace of his providence?

Pilate would know the answers and so he brings Jesus into the hall away from His accusers. Here Jesus talked freely to Pilate. Pilate was convinced that the charges were simply trumped up and the Roman government had nothing to fear from Him.

Returning to the Sanhedrin delegation, which was waiting outside the main gates of the pavement area, Pilate announced that he had found no fault with Jesus. Ordinarily this meant the prisoner was released; however, the Sanhedrin would have no part of that and continued to charge Jesus. Part of that charge was the following statement...

> "He stirreth up the people, teaching throughout all Jewry, beginning from Galilee to this place." Luke 23:5b

Galilee? Did you say Galilee? This would make Jesus a subject of Herod, the king of Galilee. Pilate could just be done with the whole thing by sending Jesus to Herod. And so, under guard, Jesus is sent across town to Herod, who was at his father's old palace. He too was in the city for the Passover celebration and many of his citizens were there as well.

Herod is in Jerusalem

Place: Jerusalem - Herod's Palace Across Town

Date: Wednesday 13 Nisan AD 30 Time: 7 AM

The streets are becoming busy, merchants are opening their businesses and already the city is astir. The soldiers holding Jesus are Romans, for Jesus' custody had been surrendered to Pilate by the temple police. The Roman soldiers move Jesus hurriedly through the streets in tight formation to prevent any mob violence.

Herod was glad to see Jesus. He had heard much about Him, he even thought that He might be John the Baptist returned to life. (Herod had John beheaded at his drunken birthday party). He hoped when he met Jesus that He would perform a miracle for him, but Jesus just stood silent before him and refused to answer him. Although Herod understood much about the Jews and their customs, he had never learned the purpose of the miracles of Christ.

Herod was undoubtedly angry with Jesus, who treated him will sullen silence. On one occasion, when the people had warned Him about Herod, Jesus called him the "old fox" and did not appear to be at all afraid of him. Herod held his temper in check, remembering his part in the death of John the Baptist. John's death still bothered him; in fact, one time he had thought that Jesus was John raised from the dead.

> "At that time Herod the tetrarch heard of the fame of Jesus, And said unto his servants, This is John the Baptist; he is risen from the dead; and therefore mighty works do show forth themselves in him." Matthew 14:1-2

Herod had never forgotten his part in the death of John the Baptist, and he was not going to make the same mistake twice.

He did allow his rough soldiers to take their pleasure in mocking and mistreating the prisoner. For even as he was questioning Jesus, the chief priests and scribes were vehemently accusing Him. Herod sent Jesus back to Pilate wearing a gorgeous robe, the robe of a king. Little did Herod know, this Man was literally King of Kings and Lord of Lords, and he was mocking Him. Herod, I feel for you on that day when you must stand in judgment before Jesus, how pitiful your robes will be to those He will wear on that day and how paltry your power compared to His.

Although Jesus had disappointed Herod, he had been well pleased that Pilate had chosen to send Jesus to him to interrogate and punish. Herod found no reason to punish Jesus, and although his soldiers had been cruel to Him, Herod releases Jesus and returns Him to Pilate under heavy guard. Neither Herod or Pilate were taking any chances of Jesus being rescued or escaping and having a riot break out in Jerusalem. Pilate was not trying to reconcile any difference between himself and Herod; he was merely trying to escape being used by Caiaphas and Annas. However, Herod had taken the whole incident differently, and Jesus was back in Pilate's hands.

Herod and Pilate were not friends before, in fact, they resented one another. Why? Because Herod believed that all the territory now ruled over by Pilate should have become his after his brother Archelaus was deposed some twenty-four years ago. Instead they appointed Roman Procurators or governors, who made their headquarters at the newly built Roman city and seaport, Caesarea.[2] Now Pilate had shown respect for Herod and his authority in Galilee and it pleased him well.

Jesus was Back Again Before Pilate

Pilate still did not want to order the execution of Jesus. Was there another way? Pilate assured the delegation that neither he nor Herod had found any fault with Jesus. The government did not have any valid reason to even try Him, let alone to execute Him.

Some of the writers indicate that the crowd had called for the release of a political prisoner. On festival days this was often done as a token of Roman good will. However, John said that it was Pilate's idea and that he had brought up the custom.

> "But ye have a custom, that I should release unto you one at the passover: will ye therefore that I release unto you the King of the Jews?" John 18:39

---

[2] Herod the Great had built the city in 26 BC. It was entirely Roman from its architecture to its temple and bathhouse.

However, both were likely correct. Someone likely mentioned the custom and Pilate immediately saw an opportunity to free Jesus. Did Pilate pick the other person in the choice? I think that he probably did, for Barabbas was indeed a wicked prisoner and one that any sane person would not want running around in the streets of Jerusalem, while Jesus was one who had shown nothing but love and compassion to the multitudes. Was Pilate ever surprised, they chose Barabbas.

You must be kidding; this man was the most popular man on the streets just four days ago on Palm Sunday. Why would they choose an evil man over Jesus? Because according to Jeremiah 17:9...

> "The heart is deceitful above all things, and desperately wicked: who can know it?" Jeremiah 17:9

Pilate gets a Note from his Wife

While they were gathering their wits, Pilate received a courier bearing a note from his wife. Her note was a warning for Pilate to have nothing to do with this just man, Jesus. Claudia must have been a very sensitive person and was well aware of the actions of the Jews. According to her note, she had *"suffered many things in a dream because of him." Matthew 27:19*

Pilate came out and assured the high priests and the gathering crowd outside the fortress that neither he nor Herod could find any fault with this just man. The events of the morning were getting around Jerusalem and the crowd was strongly dominated by well placed supporters of the high priest.

Inflamed by the supporters of the priests, the crowd called for Barabbas to be released. "What then shall I do with this man called Jesus," and they said, "Crucify Him, Crucify Him."

Hope was gone; Pilate would try one more thing. He would have Jesus scourged and perhaps that would satisfy the crowd. Scourging was extremely brutal and often deadly; the whips were called the "cat of nine tails." Nine leather straps each tipped with a pieced of metal, bone or glass were fasten to a wooden or leather braided handle. Each stroke of the whip would leave a terrible gash and some stripes cut completely to the bone.

The whipping post was a pole about eight to ten inches in diameter and about eight-foot high with a ring at the top. The whipping posts, there was more than one, were in plain view from the Pavement and from the door where the high priest and crowd were watching. The victim was stripped bare to the waist, his hands were tied and the rope went through the ring at the top of the post, the victim was then pulled up until his feet barely touched the ground. The flogging was usually at the desecration of the man with the whip, unless order otherwise. It seemed that Pilate's plan was to beat Jesus until he invoked the sympathy of the crowd.

The flogging over, the soldiers moved Jesus inside to their barracks and one or more of the soldiers platted a crown of sharp thorns, probably from the little thorn bushes used for fuel because they burned very hot. The thorns are very sharp and about one to one and a half inches long. They pushed the crown of thorns down upon the brow of Jesus. Someone found an old purple robe, the dress of a king, and put it on Jesus, meanwhile the soldiers buffeted Him with their hands.

Pilate makes a final presentation of Jesus to the crowd. The picture is awesome; He is a broken bleeding mass of humanity. The crown of thorns was a symbol of the curse brought by Adam, now the second Adam would bear them in redemption. Pilate made the presentation with just three words, *"Behold, the man."*

Still the sympathy of the crowd was not aroused, and again and again they would call for His crucifixion. The sound rang out across the cold stone payment, *"Let Him be crucified, Let Him be crucified."* Although Pilate relented to their demands, he did two things. First, he assured the high priests and the crowd that he found no fault in Jesus. Pilate was very uneasy, when he heard that Jesus said He was the Son of God. He sought the more to release Him, but the crowd would not have it. Their cries were, *"Crucify Him, Crucify Him."* Pilate saw nothing that could be done.

The high priest Caiaphas had threatened Pilate. He said he would tell Caesar that Pilate was not his friend. Pilate knew Caiaphas would carry that threat to Rome should he fail to crucify Jesus.

Seeing nothing could be done, Pilate returned to the Pavement and seated in his judgment chair, ordered the crucifixion of Jesus. It was sometime around 8:00 in the morning.

Sadly, Pilate relented to their demand. He orders the crucifixion, and then in an act that he hoped would display his innocence, he called for a basin of water and washed his hands saying, *"I am innocent of the blood of this just man."*

> "When Pilate saw that he could prevail nothing, but that rather a tumult was made, he took water, and washed his hands before the multitude, saying, I am innocent of the blood of this just person: see ye to it. Then answered all the people, and said, His blood be on us, and on our children." Matthew 27:24-25

Chapter Thirty-One

Via Dolorosa [1]

Place: Jerusalem - The Fortress Antonia   Date: Wednesday 13 Nisan AD 30
Time: Between 8 AM and 9 AM

Jesus, bearing His cross, is forced ahead of the soldiers down the street and out into the highway that leads to the place of execution. Just outside the city walls was a small hill, from the side it looked much like a human skull and so it was called "Golgotha"[2] in Hebrew and "Cavalry" in Latin. It seemed to be a common place of execution.

Whether Jesus was carrying the full cross or only the cross beam we are not sure, but since it was very heavy, more that likely He was carrying the cross on His shoulder and dragging the long post behind Him. Jesus, exhausted from a long night of interrogation,

---

[1] Means the *way of sorrows* or *the way of the cross*.

[2] "The place of the skull," either from its appearance or the fact that the skulls of previously crucified people were lying about.

several hand beatings and finally the brutal flogging this morning, was physically weak. He had already lost a lot of blood.

He stumbles and a gasp goes up from the crowd. Along the way, people are openly weeping and some are following Him along the way of sorrow. Jesus has fallen under the load of the cross.

Simon[3] a Cyrene[4] had just come in from the country and was not a part of the events of the last week, he was just looking on as a spectator, when he suddenly was forced into service. He must have looked like a strong man and so the synoptic Gospels tell us that the soldiers compelled[5] him to bear the cross for Jesus.

Jesus turns and says to the women who follow Him weeping, *"Don't weep for me but weep for yourselves and your children."* Then He spoke prophetically of the coming destruction of Jerusalem. The children of the women would be victims in that terrible time and it would have severe adverse affects on the citizens. The destruction was still forty years away but it stalked the city like a wild animal.

---

[3] Simon was an unknown person but by the time the Gospel of Mark is written both of his sons are well known in the church. (See Mark 15:21)

[4] Cyrene is a city in North Africa near modern Libya.

[5] Compel – literally at spear point.

He Carried the Cross

Soldiers are coming
    People stand aside,
Someone is being taken
    To be crucified.

The cross He carries
    Is too heavy to bear,
A thorn made crown
    Is too cruel to wear.

We're too busy to help
    Too wicked to cry,
He was carrying a cross
    On which to die.

His bloody footprints
    Left stains in the sand,
Bloody and bleeding
    Behold! The man.

He stumbles and falls
    But He makes no sound,
Pools of blood make puddles
    On the Judean ground.

A cross is being raised
    Neath a clear morning sky,
Jesus, God's son
    Is going to die.

How great that day
    When love, mercy, and grace
In Jesus our sacrifice
    Met face to face.

In the gathering dark
    Of a black Judean sky,
Jesus, our Saviour
    Would hang, bleed, and die.

Dr. Harry E. Carr
March 20, 2002

Chapter Thirty-Two

The Crucifixion

Place: The Brow of Calvary　　Date: Wednesday 13 Nisan AD 30
Time: 9 AM

The way had been long and tortuous; each footprint left behind drops of blood. At each place where they had stopped to rest, there were little pools of blood. Now they would climb the last furlong[1] to the brow on the hill.

The crosses are laying on the ground and the execution carpenter and his helpers are there. The execution squad of four soldiers was commanded by no less than a Centurion. Their principle job at the cross was to see that the execution was done and that none interfered with its process. Each man to be executed was stripped of their garments and was nailed to the cross nude. The soldiers divided the clothes into four piles; however, Jesus had a seamless

[1] A furlong was a unit of measure referred to several times in the New Testament. It is the length of a Greek stadium, which is 220 yards or 660 feet about 1/8 of a mile.

outer garment that was made of one piece. This was held on to until later since they did not want to cut or rip it. After the men were on the cross, they cast dice to see who would win the robe. In their greed and ignorance, they fulfilled the Scriptures.

> "Then the soldiers, when they had crucified Jesus, took his garments, and made four parts, to every soldier a part; and also his coat: now the coat was without seam, woven from the top throughout. They said therefore among themselves, Let us not rend it, but cast lots for it, whose it shall be: that the scripture might be fulfilled, which saith, They parted my raiment among them, and for my vesture they did cast lots. These things therefore the soldiers did." John 19:23-24

> "They part my garments among them, and cast lots upon my vesture." Psalm 22:18

While two men held the man on the cross, a nail was set somewhere in the hand and a heavy hammer drove it through into the wood. Several blows were necessary to securely fasten the nail in place. The pain was excruciating beyond words. The feet were placed together and one long nail was driven through both feet.

Jesus was nailed to the cross at nine in the morning on Wednesday. (Why Wednesday and not Friday? Because it is impossible to fulfill what Jesus said if you go with a Friday execution.)

> "For as Jonas was three days and three nights in the whale's belly; so shall the Son of man be three days and three nights in the heart of the earth." Matthew 12:40

It is totally impossible to find three days and three nights between the Friday crucifixion and the resurrection, for Jesus was raised sometime after sundown on Saturday, which is the Jewish Sunday.

The First Hours on the Cross

Place: Calvary's Hill Time: 9 AM

As Jesus was nailed to the cross that morning at nine, the first morning sacrifice was being slain in the temple area down below. It's blood splashed on the altar, while on Calvary, God's sacrifice was being killed and His blood was dripping down an old rugged cross.

The crowd had gathered around and Jesus disciples were scattered throughout the crowd, only John stood near the cross. Jesus spoke three times from the cross during the first three hours. Jesus had prayed for the forgiveness of those crucifying Him, forgave the repentant thief, and consigned His mother to the care of John.

John immediately removed Mary from the sight of the cross and Calvary's hill, taking her to his house somewhere in Jerusalem. Jesus' turning His mother over to John may not have been a long-term plan for she had sons and daughters of her own. But at this moment none are there and Jesus wished her away from the cruelty and agony of these final hours, so He had asked John to see that it was done. Jesus might have longed for her presence at the cross, for few understand the pain like a mother. However, He knew it was best for her to be away, and so in the deepest act of love and compassion, He sent her with John.

The Afternoon

As the noon hour approached so did an unusual darkness. It had come silent and quickly and seemed to grow thicker by the moment. There was no explanation, it was neither a rainstorm nor an eclipse, it lasted far too long. In the darkness, Jesus spoke His last statement. First came the sad words of Psalm 22:1.

> "My God, my God, why hast thou forsaken me?" Matthew 27:46b

The cry was followed by a cry of thirst. The soldiers had filled a sponge with vinegar (a cheap wine) and held it to His lips, but He refused to drink.

Chapter Thirty-Three

The Last Hours on Calvary

Place: Calvary's Knoll Date: Wednesday 13 Nisan AD 30
Time: 3 PM

In the shroud of darkness surrounding the knoll of Golgotha, there was the shout of victory, *"It is finished."* Jesus' hecklers had long gone away, this eerie darkness had somehow disarmed them. It was neither a storm nor night, just thick black darkness. They had melted away and disappeared into it the shadows of the darkness and found their way home.

Only the soldiers and a few of Jesus' disciples were huddled in the darkness. Three women waited in the long darkness near the cross, Mary Magdalene, Mary the mother of James the less, and Salome the mother of James and John. At last it was over, Jesus bowed His head and said, *"Father into thy hands I commend my spirit"* and slipped silently into eternity.

It was the 9th hour or 3:00 in the afternoon; down below in the city the lamb of the evening sacrifice was shedding its blood at the great altar, while God's lamb was dying on Calvary's hill. The earth shuddered as its Creator died. The earthquake was severe, rocks were broken and some of the stones were shifted away from the nearby graves. The graves were opened and some of the saints, although we are not told which ones, came out of the grave and appeared to many within the holy city. However, they did not come out of the grave until after Jesus came out of the tomb. Jesus was the very first person to be resurrected from the dead.

The witness of Christ was strong at Calvary. The execution squad was impressed by what they had seen, heard, and experienced that day. The Centurion commanding the execution squad and every soldier with him said, *"Truly this was the Son of God."*

The great veil in the temple that separated the priest and people from the presence of a holy God was rent from the top to the bottom. Access to the presence of God was now available to every believer.

> "Having therefore, brethren, boldness to enter into the holiest by the blood of Jesus, By a new and living way, which he hath consecrated for us, through the veil, that is to say, his flesh;" Hebrews 10:19-20

The darkness had lifted as miraculously as it came, shadows became shapes and shapes were people. The two thieves were still alive. A courier arrived from Pilate, the Sanhedrin had requested that Pilate expedite the executions. In compliance, the Centurion ordered the legs of all those crucified to be broken. The soldiers made short, quick work of the assignment. The sound of breaking bones and the scream of the thieves would break the silence.

One soldier accompanying the three on the detail was armed with a short javelin. Its wide sharp blade gleamed in the returning light as he passed Jesus, who was already dead. He thrust the spear into the side of Jesus, whose body was already stretched to its limits on the cross. The javelin sliced through His side leaving a gaping hole, the size of a man's hand. All the accumulation of blood and liquids in his lungs and chest capacity came gushing out. Jesus was certainly dead; there was no need to break His legs.

Joseph, A Friend of Jesus

Joseph, a man of Arimathæa, was born and raised in the village of Arimathea, located about two hours north of Jerusalem. In Old Testament times the village was called Ramah and was the home of Samuel the prophet. Joseph, like many wealthy Jews, had a residence in Jerusalem and had built his family tomb in a garden just outside the city gates. This was the place all Jews wanted to be buried, for they knew that the Messiah, when He came in His glory, would come through the Eastern Gate and they wanted to be there to greet Him.

Joseph was both a wealthy man and an influential member of the Jewish Sanhedrin Court. Joseph had trusted in Christ as the

Messiah, but he had not been open about his faith. For fear of the Jews, he had kept his discipleship secret.

Joseph now steps forward as a true disciple. I don't know if it was his idea or another's, but he proposed to bury the body of Jesus. The bodies of the criminals were considered the property of the state; therefore, before he could take the body from the cross, he must have the permission of Pilate.

Joseph leaves Calvary and heads for the Praetorium, which was located next door to the temple. Pilate was in, and yes, he would see Joseph, not knowing what this influential man might want. We can only imagine how surprised Pilate must have been when he asked for the release of the body of Jesus. Pilate marveled too, that Jesus was already dead. He had only been on the cross six hours; usually it took two or three days for a man to die. Pilate had already sent a courier to the Centurion with special instructions to speed the death of those on the cross, but this was much too soon. Before he would release the body, he must have a certifiable death announcement from the Centurion of the execution squad.

It is now nearing 4:00 PM when the courier leaves the Governor's office headed for the hill of Calvary. The journey would take about thirty or forty minutes, while Joseph could do nothing until he waited for Pilate's answer.

Pilate Releases the Body of Jesus

The Centurion came personally to make his report to Pilate. He rehearses the events of the last hour, the breaking of the legs of the thieves and the javelin thrust into the side of Jesus. Jesus was certifiably dead. Accepting the report of the Centurion, Pilate releases the body of Jesus to Joseph.

Joseph was now free to begin the burial process. The hour is growing late, all this activity had taken much time and the hour to get Jesus into the grave was short indeed. They had perhaps just a little over an hour to complete the burial.

Laid to Rest

Place: Jerusalem – Calvary and the Nearby Garden Tomb
Date: Wednesday 13 Nisan AD 30

Joseph finds Nicodemus, and together they gather the burial material. Most Jews kept burial spices in their home. It was an expensive burial spice, spikenard, which Mary had poured on Jesus just last Saturday night at the feast in Bethany. Jesus would be buried in his new tomb, located in a garden only a hundred or so yards from the place where He had been crucified.

The servants of Joseph and Nicodemus lifted the cross from its socket in the stones of the hillside. Gently the cross was laid down and with care the nails must have been pulled from His hands and feet. Loving hands would carry the body to Joseph's new tomb. The body would be washed as clean as possible and then wrapped in linen, wound from foot to the head. Spices would be poured or laid on the linen and then another piece of linen was wound in the opposite direction, binding both hands and feet. Finally, more spices and more linen until it was inches deep.

Last of all, a piece of cloth called a *napkin* was put over the head and tied under the chin to keep the mouth closed. The face was left open. Now the body was laid on the slab specially prepared for it, and at last, the door is closed and sealed into place.

The sun had slipped behind the western hills, shadows gathered across Jerusalem, and the evening breeze from the Mediterranean was coming up to Jerusalem across the plains of Sharon. The darkness of the tomb was made even darker by the evening shadows. Time was of an essence to this crew; they must have the massive door of the tomb rolled closed within the next few minutes. The high day of preparation would begin with the darkness of today. Everyone hurried and soon the heavy stone started rolling down the stone track. In the darkness, small pieces of gravel lying in the stone track made loud noises as they were crunched beneath the enormous weight of the stone door as it rolled into place. The sun was set, Jerusalem lay bathed in darkness as they made their way home.

Jesus now rests in Joseph's new tomb, and thus the Scriptures were fulfilled.

"And he made his grave with the wicked, and with the rich in his death;" Isaiah 53:9a

The Women at the Grave Site

Place: Jerusalem - In the Garden Near the Tomb of Jesus

Watching in the growing shadows of darkness, were the women who had come down from Galilee with Jesus and His disciples. They watched the final preparation, marked the tomb in their minds, and made plans to come to the tomb as soon as the Passover and Sabbath were past.

Part Two

The Resurrection

Three Old Crooked and Rusty Nails

Three old crooked and rusty nails
    Useless now they were cast aside,
Their bent shafts stained with blood
    Here Jesus had been crucified.

Nails that once held the Son of God
    Fastened to an old and rugged tree,
They pierced His hands and His feet
    Jesus wore those nails for one like me.

Precious nails they are to me,
    Nails of love and nails of duty
In His hands, they are forever,
    Objects of love, grace, and beauty.

Dr. Harry E. Carr
March 9, 2002

The Resurrection

Chapter Thirty-Four

The Resurrection and its Importance

The bodily resurrection of Jesus from the dead is essential to the Christian faith. Paul wrote...

> "Now if Christ be preached that he rose from the dead, how say some among you that there is no resurrection of the dead? But if there be no resurrection of the dead, then is Christ not risen: And if Christ be not risen, then is our preaching vain, and your faith is also vain. Yea, and we are found false witnesses of God; because we have testified of God that he raised up Christ: whom he raised not up, if so be that the dead rise not. For if the dead rise not, then is not Christ raised: And if Christ be not raised, your faith is vain; ye are yet in your sins. Then they also which are fallen asleep in Christ are perished. If in this life only we have hope in Christ, we are of all men most miserable. But now is Christ risen from the dead, and become the firstfruits of them that slept." I Corinthians 15:12-20

Jesus' resurrected body was a body of flesh and bone. His own testimony regarding this is given in Luke.

> "But they [the Apostles] were terrified and affrighted, and supposed that they had seen a spirit. And he [Jesus] said unto them, Why are ye troubled? and why do thoughts arise in your

> hearts? Behold my hands and my feet, that it is I myself: handle me, and see; for a spirit hath not flesh and bones, as ye see me have. And when he had thus spoken, he showed them his hands and his feet." Luke 24:37-40

Even though they could see that Jesus' body was indeed flesh and bone, He gave them further evidence that left no question that His body was real.

> "And while they yet believed not for joy, and wondered, he said unto them, Have ye here any meat? And they gave him a piece of a broiled fish, and of an honeycomb. And he took it, and did eat before them." Luke 24:41-43

The following narrative will attempt to put in order the appearances of Jesus and examine the infallible proofs of the bodily resurrection. The event and the witnesses will join in the narrative. I will make every attempt to let you see the reality of the Resurrection through the eyes of those who actually saw and touched Jesus and who interacted with Him in a way which established beyond any doubt that His body was one of flesh and bone.

I am always asked, "Did Jesus' resurrected body have blood?" Well, flesh and bone requires bodily fluid! The blood of Adam was no doubt good until that fateful day in Eden, when in disobedience, he ate of the forbidden fruit. From that moment on, he had a fallen nature which through his blood, would be transmitted to all his descendants except one. [1]

The precious blood of Jesus was given in sacrifice for all those who would believe, and was presented by the risen Jesus on the Great Altar in Heaven. However, I believe that the resurrected body, to function as a human body, must have restored blood just as it had restored flesh and bone. Jesus was not a bloodless being with neither color nor bodily function, to prove this, Jesus ate with the disciples on more than one occasion.

It is my sincere hope that as you read this narrative, you too will see Jesus through the eyes of these witnesses and reach the conclusion that the evidence of His Resurrection was so established in and by His appearances, that it constituted **infallible proof** of the bodily resurrection of Jesus. The believer has a risen Christ, who is alive forever more with salvation and life for all who will believe. The conclusion of Luke in Acts chapter one is the conclusion of this author without reservation.

> "Until the day in which he [Jesus] was taken up, after that he through the Holy Ghost had given commandments unto the apostles whom he had chosen: **To whom also he showed himself alive after his passion by many infallible proofs,** being seen of them forty days, and speaking of the things pertaining to the kingdom of God:" Acts 1:2-3

---

[1] That one was Jesus, who was virgin born without a human father. He did not receive the sin nature of Adam; His blood was the precious blood of God.

Remembering

Place: Jerusalem | Date: 15 Nisan AD 30

Time: Thursday Morning

It has been an exceptionally long weekend for the disciples. John had taken Jesus' mother to his house in Jerusalem and apparently Peter was staying there as well. Other disciples were staying with relatives in Jerusalem; however, it does seem that the bulk of the disciples were staying in the suburb of Bethany. They were probably staying with Martha, Mary, Lazarus, or even Simon, who had been healed of leprosy by Jesus. It may seem strange that Salome and James stayed in Bethany rather than at John's house, but then again Bethany seemed to be a safe distance from the tumult of Jerusalem. Some may have also stayed in the little suburb of Bethphage.

Most of the disciples were from Galilee, but they could not return home until Sunday. Travel on the Sabbath day was limited to two thousand cubits or about three thousand feet, which is just over half a mile. The journey back home would take, at the least, two or more days.

Scattered Sheep

Place: Jerusalem

Date: 14 Nisan AD 30

Time: Tuesday Night

Jesus had said the following to the disciples in the upper room at the Last Supper...

> "Then saith Jesus unto them, All ye shall be offended because of me this night: for it is written, I will smite the shepherd, and the sheep of the flock shall be scattered abroad. But after I am risen again, I will go before you into Galilee." Matthew 26:31-32

The apostles and many of the disciples were nearby, all that is, except Judas Iscariot, the traitor. Filled with unremitting remorse, he had returned the thirty silver coins to the priests. When they had refused them, Judas cast them into the temple. Finding a tree over the valley of Hinnom, he hanged himself. Falling into the valley below, he burst asunder.

> "Then Judas, which had betrayed him, when he saw that he was condemned, repented himself, and brought again the thirty pieces of silver to the chief priests and elders, Saying, I have sinned in that I have betrayed the innocent blood. And they said, What is that to us? see thou to that. And he cast down the pieces of silver in the temple, and departed, and went and hanged himself." Matthew 27:3-5

> "Men and brethren, this scripture must needs have been fulfilled, which the Holy Ghost by the mouth of David spake before concerning Judas, which was guide to them that took Jesus. For he was numbered with us, and had obtained part of this ministry. Now this man purchased a field with the reward of iniquity; and falling headlong, he burst asunder in the midst, and all his bowels gushed out." Acts 1:16-18

The Resurrection

Chapter Thirty-Five

Remembering the Remarkable Jesus

Place: Jerusalem Time: After the Crucifixion, the Disciples Remember Galilee

The wait was long and their doubts and fears were real, they too might become victims of the high priests. If they wanted to remove every trace of Jesus and His followers, then they too might be hunted down and killed by the temple authorities.

Jesus' Power Over Nature

Place: Galilee Time: During the Days of Jesus' Ministry

Everyone seemed to have forgotten all of Jesus' promises; their hopes had been crushed on Calvary's hill. Jesus was dead, the ministry was over, and they would soon return to their nets and businesses. But they would never forget those days by the seashore of Galilee, when His voice rang out over the hillside and people were astonished at His doctrine.

They would definitely not forget that stormy night on the Sea of Galilee when they were sure that they would perish, but Jesus spoke to the wind and the sea and they obeyed His voice. They had remarked among themselves, "*What manner of man is this, that even the winds and sea obey him!*" *Matthew 8:27b*

Jesus' Power Over Death

Place: Nain Time: In the Early Days of Jesus' Ministry

Many of Jesus' disciples had been with Him when He entered into the little mountain town of Nain, a village about five or six miles southwest of Nazareth. A funeral procession was winding its way through the streets toward the village cemetery. The young man on the bier was the only son of a widowed mother. Moved in deep compassion Jesus commanded the procession to stop, then at Jesus' word, the young man is restored to life and returned to his mother.

Place: Capernaum Time: During One of Jesus' Visits to the City

The apostles and some disciples were present when Jairus, the ruler of the synagogue at Capernaum, came seeking Jesus because his little daughter was very ill. While they went toward his house, servants brought news that she had passed away and advised Jairus not to trouble Jesus any further. How little they knew about Jesus. The yard was full of mourners, but Jesus calmly took Peter,

James, John, and the parents into the house and called Jairus' daughter back from the dead. What a scene it had been, Jairus, his wife, and his little daughter standing outside the house, waving goodbye to Jesus as they merged back into the city.

Place: Bethany - Just Outside of Jerusalem Time: About Two Weeks Ago

Every one of them had been at Bethany where just a week ago, Jesus had called Lazarus from the tomb after he had been dead for four days. What a stir this had caused! The enemies of Jesus had sprung into action. Never mind the miracle, never mind the power of God, never mind the joy of Martha and Mary, they were determined to kill this man called Jesus.

They knew that Jesus had power over death while he was alive, but He was dead. Those lips could no longer call the dead back to life. His voice was silent, He was gone, and only the echo remained in their hearts. Oh! How they wished He walked among them again.

The sadness just would not go away. The awful agony of Jesus' suffering and death on the cross was still fresh on the mind of every disciple. How could they do this to a good man like Jesus? There seemed to be no justice in Jerusalem. Behind the whole thing had been the men who walked in the robes of the priesthood.

The Resurrection

Chapter Thirty-Six

A Borrowed Grave

Every grave of every believer is only borrowed. You may have it back after the resurrection. Jesus opened the way for this victory. He would borrow a grave, but only for three days, and it would sanctify that spot of ground forever. Here the body of Jesus slept for three crucial days, and here victory over death was won forever and ever.

Place: Calvary & the Nearby Garden Outside Jerusalem   Date: 14 Nisan AD 30

Joseph of Arimathaea[1] and his friend Nicodemus[2] of Jerusalem, both disciples of Jesus and members of the Sanhedrin Court, had

[1]Arimathaea is a small Jewish village about twenty miles northwest of Jerusalem. Joseph, like many Jews of his day, probably had a home within the city limits of Jerusalem. He certainly planned to be buried there.

[2] Nicodemus met Jesus in John 3 and became a disciple but not openly, neither was Joseph's conversion commonly known. Both of these men were members of the Sanhedrin Court; however, neither had consented to the death of Jesus and had no part in the dastardly plans formed by the leadership of that court.

taken Jesus' body from the cross and laid it in Joseph's new garden tomb. The women at the cross followed and had marked well the garden grave in their minds as well as in their hearts.

> "And, behold, there was a man named Joseph, a counsellor; and he was a good man, and a just: (The same had not consented to the counsel and deed of them;) he was of Arimathaea, a city of the Jews: who also himself waited for the kingdom of God. This man went unto Pilate, and begged the body of Jesus. And he took it down, and wrapped it in linen, and laid it in a sepulchre that was hewn in stone, wherein never man before was laid. And that day was the preparation, and the sabbath drew on. And the women also, which came with him from Galilee, followed after, and beheld the sepulchre, and how his body was laid. And they returned, and prepared spices and ointments; and rested the sabbath day according to the commandment." Luke 23:50-56

A Roman Seal and a Roman Guards

Place: The Garden Tomb Date: 14 Nisan AD 30

Time: Nearing Dark

The Roman guards had been posted at the garden tomb just after dark on the day of the crucifixion. A bright Roman Government seal marked the fact that the stone was in place, and the guards were there to see that the seal was never broken.

These guards had been a complimentary detachment assigned by Pilate at the request of the high priests. They were taking no chances that the disciples might steal the body and claim a resurrection. You see, the enemy had not forgotten Jesus' claim that He would raise from the dead. They had won a victory, Jesus was dead and they were determined to see that He remained entombed forever. For you see, these men were Sadducees and they did not believe in the resurrection of the dead.

Place: Jerusalem - John's House

John had taken Jesus' mother, Mary, to his house from the cross before Jesus died. She would not return to Nazareth until after the Passover. After the death of Jesus, Peter stumbled through the streets of Jerusalem blindly with his load of guilt. Perhaps the eyes of Jesus still burned in his mind, for on his third denial, Jesus had turned and looked right at him. Peter had left the scene weeping bitterly.

> "And the Lord turned, and looked upon Peter. And Peter remembered the word of the Lord, how he had said unto him, Before the cock crow, thou shalt deny me thrice. And Peter went out, and wept bitterly." Luke 22:61-62

It was probably on purpose that Peter arrived at the home of John seeking his companionship. John must have persuaded him to stay with him through the Passover and the Sabbath. The other apostles were scattered throughout the city of Jerusalem and in the nearby villages of Bethany and Bethphage. Here they would be waiting for the three days to end and the new week to begin. Thursday had been the day of high preparation.

> "The Jews therefore, because it was the preparation, that the bodies should not remain upon the cross on the sabbath day, (for that sabbath day was an high day,) besought Pilate that their legs might be broken, and that they might be taken away." John 19:31

Friday had been the Passover and of course, Saturday was the regular Sabbath. When Sunday morning came, they would begin the long walk back to Galilee.

Dreading the Walk Back to Galilee

None would look forward to the walk home. Jesus was gone, but every place along the pilgrim road would have memories for them, Jericho where Zacchaeus was saved, and the ruins of old Jericho with its farm markets and beggars, would recall that day when blind Bartimaeus called out to the passing Jesus and his sight was restored and that of his friend as well. The rich young ruler, who had turned sorrowfully away, would come back to memory. Would they see him again? If so, they would tell him the sad story about Jesus. The road home would come alive with memories, precious memories that would challenge their faith.

Vanishing Hopes

They had arrived in Jerusalem only a few days ago with such high hopes, which had been reinforced with Palm Sunday. Jesus was certainly popular on that day; they had welcomed Him in fulfillment of the sayings of Zechariah.

> "Rejoice greatly, O daughter of Zion; shout, O daughter of Jerusalem: behold, thy King cometh unto thee: he is just, and having salvation; lowly, and riding upon an ass, and upon a colt the foal of an ass." Zechariah 9:9

The Resurrection

Chapter Thirty-Seven

The Early Morning Visit to the Graveyard

Place: Jerusalem — Date: Easter Sunday 17 Nisan AD 30

Time: Before Daylight

This morning several ladies, who had been waiting for the Sabbath to end, gathered their burial spices, sponges, water, and cloths and headed for the tomb. One more time they would look on that beloved face of Jesus. He was their Messiah, their hope, and their dream of redemption, but He was dead. Only last week, they had been present with Jesus on the pilgrimage to Jerusalem. They had shared as much as possible with Him and the apostles on those brief days prior to the Passover. They had been eyewitnesses of His miracles enroute to Jerusalem. They had shared the joy of Palm Sunday and had wept openly as they led Jesus carrying His cross to Calvary.

Committed Women on the Way to the Garden

These women ought to be decorated for their heroic attempt to make sure that the body of Jesus was properly prepared for His burial. They had to wait until the Sabbath was ended, and still finish the matter in time to join the caravan that would be headed home to Galilee. We must admire their devotion, courage, and determination. Who were these women?

At least two and maybe more will remain anonymous. We can only report the names given to us in the Gospels. Matthew names only two ladies, Mary Magdalene and the other Mary, which would have been the wife of Cleophas and the mother of James and Joses. Mark mentions these two and adds the name of Salome, the wife of Zebedee and mother of James and John.

Luke adds the name of Joanna[1] and said that there were other women there also that had come with Him out of Galilee. John adds nothing to the list, telling the story as he heard it from Mary Magdalene. These had been the same ladies that were at the cross when Jesus died and had watched the burial in the garden tomb. They were witnesses of Jesus' death and burial and now would be witnesses of the Resurrection as well.

---

[1] Joanna was the wife of Chuza, the steward (treasurer of finances) of King Herod who ruled over Galilee. She probably lived in the city of Tiberas on Lake Galilee. She is mentioned only twice and both times by Luke; however, she was likely one of the women who stayed by the cross and witnessed the death and burial of Jesus.

What Do You Talk About on the Way to a Graveyard?

Can you imagine the conversation on this morning as the women chattered in the dark? Their talk had come partly out of loneliness, partly out of love, and some out of fear. Sometimes those things loosen our tongues like nothing else. We talk because we are nervous or because we don't like what we know is going to happen. Most of their words are lost in the morning breeze coming up from the Mediterranean and across the fields of Sharon, where the lily of the valley would be blooming.

A Heavy Stone and a Roman Guard

We do know that their conversation finally came around to the heavy stone that had been rolled to cover the doorway of the tomb. How would they ever be able to move the stone? They could expect no help from the Roman soldiers. Even if they permitted them in the tomb, they would not give them aid nor would they break that highly visible Roman seal for their benefit.

A Tremor in the Night

The ladies were not expecting the unexpected. One wonders why they kept going, knowing that they could not move the stone. The earthquake in the night had been more like a tremor; no one seemed to recall it. There had been an earth-shaking earthquake on Wednesday afternoon, was this an aftershock? The Bible says it was a great earthquake. Was it great in velocity or great in what it accomplished?

The Angel Sent by the Lord

Place: At the Garden Tomb Date: Sunday 17 Nisan AD 30
Time: In the Dark Night Hours Long before Dawn

The angel of the Lord sent from heaven used the earthquake to roll away the stone from the entrance into the tomb. Almost casually, the angel set upon the stone and allowed the Roman soldiers to see him. The angel's brilliant countenance was brighter than a lightning bolt and his raiment was white as snow. Fear does strange things to people. It caused these hardened, fearless, fighting solders to simply shake themselves into a dead faint. They were out cold, probably for several minutes, and when they came to, they did not see the angel, but the stone was moved. Whether they looked into the tomb or not, we are not told, but they were confident that the body was gone.

What had they seen? Would anyone believe that they had seen an angel? Would they dare tell anyone that they were so scared that they blacked out? Certainly they would not report it to their centurion, and they would hope that it would never come to the ears of Pontius Pilate, because if it did, they were dead men.

The Roman Soldiers Flee the Garden

Sometime during the darkness, the soldiers fled from the garden tomb. They headed not for the fortress Antonia, where their superiors were, but for the house of the high priest with their reports.

A conference was called; the spiritual side of the story was easily dismissed by the most liberal of religious men. They believed in neither the Bible nor angels, and they absolutely could not see God's hand in this.

Fabricating a Lie and Paying a Bribe

Something had to be done and it had to be done quickly. They must get their story on the street before daylight this morning. What could they say? What would people believe? The priests and elders gave the soldiers the lie.

> "Saying, Say ye, His disciples came by night, and stole him away while we slept." Matthew 28:13

Of course, derelict of duty was an offense punishable by death. If the authorities heard of this, they were all in big trouble. However, the chief priests and elders assured them that if it came to the ear of the authorities, they would take care of the matter. Hadn't they threatened Pilate into crucifying Jesus? Perhaps they could? A very large bribe was given to the soldiers. How much? We are not told, only that it was a large sum of money.

They took the money and the promise of protection and went out telling the lie made up by the chief priests and elders. It was a lie that many might want to believe and it found common acceptance among the Jews for years after the Resurrection.

An Empty Garden and an Open Tomb

When the ladies arrived, the Roman soldiers were nowhere in sight and the enormous stone covering the door of the sepulchre had been rolled away. The whole scene - the gaping black hole into the tomb, the missing Roman soldiers, and the heavy stone set back to its original position disturbed Mary Magdalene. Something was dreadfully wrong here.

Mary Magdalene Runs to Get Help

Place: In Jerusalem at John's House

They needed help and she knew exactly where Peter and John were staying, almost everyone did, since they were regarded as leaders among the apostles. Leaving the other women behind, she fled down the road to John's house. Arriving breathless, she shouted...

> "They have taken away the Lord out of the sepulchre, and we know not where they have laid him." John 20:2b

Mary had not seen nor heard the angels. She only knew that the stone was moved and the soldiers were gone. She was also sure that the body was moved in the night without their knowledge.

With the Other Ladies at the Open Tomb

The other ladies remained behind. Moving closer, they peered into the grave. It would seem, by the accounts given that only one angel had brought the earthquake and rolled away the stone. He apparently sat upon it until the guards, who were rendered as dead men, recovered and fled the scene. He was joined my another angel and then both angels reappeared inside the tomb.

Cautiously, the women entered the tomb. Two angels in white apparel were inside the tomb. Such a sight must have struck terror into the hearts of this little group of women. One angel spoke...

> "Fear not ye: for we know that ye seek Jesus, which was crucified. He is not here: for he has risen, as he said. Come, see the place where the lord lay. And go quickly, and tell his disciples that he is risen from the dead;" Matthew 28:5b-7a

Leaving the tomb, the ladies may have divided into groups, because the apostles and disciples must have been scattered throughout the city and its suburbs of Bethany and Bethphage in private homes.

Peter and John Come Running

Remember, Mary's report was not about a risen Saviour, but about a grave robbing.

> "They have taken away the Lord out of the sepulchre, and we know not where they have laid him." John 20:2b

Peter and John race to the tomb. John, perhaps the younger, won the race; however, he did not enter the tomb, but waited for Peter. Together they entered the tomb and saw nothing except the grave clothes and the napkin that had been around Jesus' head folded and laying by itself. This was enough for John. From that moment, he believed that Jesus had risen from the dead.

> "Peter therefore went forth, and that other disciple, and came to the sepulchre. So they ran both together: and the other disciple did outrun Peter, and came first to the sepulchre. And he stooping down, and looking in, saw the linen clothes lying; yet went he not in. Then cometh Simon Peter following him, and went into the sepulchre, and seeth the linen clothes lie, And the napkin, that was about his head, not lying with the linen clothes, but wrapped together in a place by itself. Then went in also that other disciple, which came first to the sepulchre, and he saw, and believed. For as yet they knew not the scripture, that he must rise again from the dead. Then the disciples went away again unto their own home." John 20:3-10

Peter and John saw nothing further that they could do at the tomb and started back to John's house. It is apparent that they must have passed Mary Magdalene on her way back to the tomb. The first gray light of dawn was stealing over the eastern mountains of Moab, when Mary reached the little garden and the empty tomb.

Peter and John must have told Mary of their findings when they passed her on the road, for she knew the body of Jesus was gone.

The Resurrection

Chapter Thirty-Eight

Mary Magdalene – The First Recorded Appearance of the Risen Christ

Place: Jerusalem, at the Garden Tomb Date: Easter Sunday 17 Nisan AD 30
Time: The Early Morning Dawn

Mary Magdalene arrives at the tomb, alone and weeping. The news of Peter and John had brought her no comfort, for they had no idea what had happened to the body. Well, John might have had, but he may not have shared the thought that he believed that Jesus had risen from the dead.

Holding to the stone walls of the tomb, Mary peers into the darkness beyond the open door. There was a strange light inside; the apparel of the angels must have radiated a soft white light. One angel set at the head of the grave slab and the other at the foot. They asked only one question, *"Woman, why weepest thou?"* Literally, "Lady, what are you crying about?" She explained...

> "Because they have taken away my Lord, and I know not where they have laid him." John 20:13b

It was a time for rejoicing not weeping, but she did not yet know the great news nor did the angels tell her. Doesn't it surprise you that she seemed to have no fear of these beings in white apparel? Her heart was set on something far more important than her fear. Where was the body of Jesus?

Hearing someone in the garden behind her, Mary looked back over her shoulder and saw the outline of a man standing among the shadows. Supposing Him to be only Joseph of Arimathæa's gardener, His question posed no threat, for He asked the same question posed by the angels.

> "Woman, why weepest thou? Whom seekest thou?" John 20:15b

Was there something familiar about that voice? No, there was no way that it could be Jesus, for He was dead and buried somewhere. It was not His presence she sought, but a dead body. Now she asked the person whom she supposed was the gardener...

> "Sir, if thou have borne him hence, tell me where thou hast laid him, and I will take him away." John 20:15d

Had the gardener moved the body of Jesus? This was sometimes done to prepare the slab for the next family burial. Had he re-interned Jesus somewhere else? It was highly unlikely that it had been done this quickly, but totally possible.

Snapped Back to Reality

In Mary's mind, Jesus was still dead. Only the voice behind her snapped her back to reality. *"Mary,"* she had heard that voice many times. The first time she had heard it was when He had set her free from seven devils that possessed her. How many times since that first meeting had she heard that voice, for she had often been among the ladies that sometimes traveled to religious gatherings with Jesus.

> "Now when Jesus was risen early the first day of the week, he appeared first to Mary Magdalene, out of whom he had cast seven devils." Mark 16:9

All doubt fled from her mind. Jesus was alive! He had risen from the dead, just as He had said! The title she knew Him by came like a shout of joy from her lips, *"Rabboni"* (master).

Touch Me Not

The next words of Jesus to Mary are usually misunderstood, and therefore misinterpreted.

> "Jesus saith unto her, Touch me not; for I am not yet ascended to my Father: but go to my brethren, and say unto them, I ascend unto my Father, and your Father; and to my God, and your God." John 20:17

The normal interpretation of this is somewhat like this, *"Now Mary, a new relationship exists between us. You must not hold on to me anymore."* I find such an interpretation rather silly, since in the next appearance of Jesus, the women hold Him by the feet without any comment from Jesus and later He even invites His disciples to touch His hands and feet. Still yet, a week later He invites the unbelieving apostle Thomas to thrust his hand into His side.

No, Jesus must mean something else in His statement to Mary. Notice carefully the language. It is the language of the high priest preparing to officiate in his official capacity, *"My Father, your Father, my God, your God."*

The Parallel of the Day of Atonement

On the Day of Atonement (Yom Kippur) the high priest first prepared himself by washing and offering a sacrifice for himself and his family first. From this point, the high priest could touch no one nor could anyone touch him, until the atonement was finished.

Blood Sprinkled on the Mercy Seat

Deep within the tabernacle or temple was the holiest place of all, and in that cubical space set the symbol of Israel, the Ark of the Covenant. It was a gold covered wood box that was 2½ cubits (45 inches) long by 1½ cubits (27 inches) wide and 1½ cubits (27 inches) high. Inside the box were the two tablets of the Ten Commandments, a golden pot of manna, and Aaron's rod that budded. The lid of the box was covered with beaten gold and called the Mercy Seat. Two golden cherubim angels hovered over the lid with outstretched wings. Between those wings dwelled the

"Shekinah" [1] presence of God. The high priest carrying the shed blood of the sacrifice of the atonement passed beyond the curtain out of sight of all. Here seven times he sprinkled the blood upon the Mercy Seat and the atonement was made.

Jesus on His Way to the Great Tabernacle in Heaven

That morning, Jesus must have been on His way to the Great Tabernacle in Heaven, bearing His own precious blood He shed at Calvary to make atonement for our sins forever. Until this was finished, none could touch Him. This must have been accomplished in the space and time between this meeting with Mary Magdalene and the next appearance to the women somewhere on the road between Jerusalem and Bethany.

> "Neither by the blood of goats and calves, but by his own blood he entered in once into the holy place, having obtained eternal redemption for us." Hebrews 9:12

[1] The *shekinah* presence of God was some type of cloud that hovered over the altar and between the wings of the cherubim angels. It signified the holy presence of God.

Women on the Way to Bethany - The Second Recorded Appearance of Jesus

Place: The Bethany - Jerusalem Road Date: Easter Sunday 17 Nisan AD 30
Time: Sometime Later in the Morning

The urgent news given by the angels at the tomb had scattered the women that had remained behind. There were several places they must go, and they must do it before everyone left for Galilee.

After Mary Magdalene left to get the apostles, the only women left at the tomb were Mary the mother of James, Salome, Joanna, and two others. They divided into groups to go give the apostles and disciples the message of the angels. They probably suspected that they would not be believed, so they did not go alone but took support. Matthew alone tells us about this casual meeting of Jesus on the road to Bethany.

> "And they departed quickly from the sepulchre with fear and great joy; and did run to bring his disciples word. And as they went to tell his disciples, behold, Jesus met them, saying, All hail. And they came and held him by the feet, and worshipped him. Then said Jesus unto them, Be not afraid: go tell my brethren that they go into Galilee, and there shall they see me." Matthew 28:8-10

How Many Women were at the Meeting?

Most people, and even I, have assumed that there were only two women on the road to Bethany. The only reason to believe this is because Matthew named only two as being at the sepulchre;

however, it would be an error to consider that, for one of those named was Mary Magdalene and we know that she had went to get Peter and John and was not with them. It might have been any combination of the number of women listed. Since Mary Magdalene was gone when the angels appeared, there remained among the named women, Salome, Joanna, and Mary the wife of Celophas, who had heard the message of the angels at the tomb; however, there were two or more other unnamed women with them. Mary, the wife of Celophas, apparently was not among those who saw Jesus on the road, she may have gone to one of the other destinations. Did the disciples discredit in their mind what she had seen? It is apparent that Mary still had doubt about the resurrection on the road home to Emmaus.

So there might have been five or six or even more in the group; but more than likely they had divided up to get the message quickly to the disciples. Some disciples were in Jerusalem and others were in Bethany and Bethphage.

It is an undisclosed number on the road to Bethany, but there were at least two or three, if not more of them. Luke only reports that they went and told the disciples.

Behold

"And as they went to tell his disciples, **behold,** Jesus met them, saying, All hail. And they came and held him by the feet, and worshipped him. Then said Jesus unto them, Be not afraid: go tell my brethren that they go into Galilee, and there shall they see me." Matthew 28:9-10

"Behold," what a word to announce this spectacular meeting. Behold or make known indeed that this was Jesus, and they lost no opportunity doing so. They came and held Him by the feet, those awful scars of crucifixion must have stared up at them. Yes indeed this was Jesus and He was alive. There was no rebuke from Jesus as they held His feet and worshipped Him. The blood was sprinkled on the altar of heaven, and now they could handle Him and see that it was really Jesus, the same Jesus that was risen from the dead.

Jesus renewed the message first given by the angels to the disciples about a meeting in Galilee. Did the women get the message wrong or did Jesus feel it was important to get the disciples out of Jerusalem? We may not know; however, we do know that He met with them in a great number in Galilee. Was the message for the many disciples in Jerusalem that He would not be able to meet with because of the temple authorities but would meet them in Galilee? Since the meetings in Jerusalem were limited as to the number of people in them, we don't know. We can only repeat His message, but apparently the disciples understood.

A Private Meeting with Peter in Jerusalem – The Third Recorded Appearance of Jesus

Place: Somewhere in Jerusalem Date: 17 Nisan AD 30

Time: Sunday Afternoon

Mark indicates that the message of the angels was somewhat longer than the reports of others. In a comparison of the message of the angels in all four Gospels, we see Peter's name is mentioned only in Mark's account.

> "And the angel answered and said unto the women, Fear not ye: for I know that ye seek Jesus, which was crucified. **He is not here: for he is risen, as he said. Come, see the place where the Lord lay. And go quickly, and tell his disciples that he is risen from the dead; and, behold, he goeth before you into Galilee; there shall ye see him: lo, I have told you.** And they departed quickly from the sepulchre with fear and great joy; and did run to bring his disciples word." Matthew 28:5-8

> "And it came to pass, as they were much perplexed thereabout, behold, two men stood by them in shining garments: And as they were afraid, and bowed down their faces to the earth, they said unto them, **Why seek ye the living among the dead? He is not here, but is risen: remember how he spake unto you when he was yet in Galilee, Saying, The Son of man must be delivered into the hands of sinful men, and be crucified, and the third day rise again.** And they remembered his words," Luke 24:4-8

> "And entering into the sepulchre, they saw a young man sitting on the right side, clothed in a long white garment; and they were affrighted. And he saith unto them, **Be not affrighted: Ye seek Jesus of Nazareth, which was crucified: he is risen; he is not here: behold the place where they laid him. But go your way, tell his disciples and Peter that he goeth before you into Galilee: there shall ye see him, as he said unto you.**" Mark 16:5-7

In John's Gospel, the only reported message is just four words and they were spoken to Mary Magdalene long after the others had departed.

> "And seeth two angels in white sitting, the one at the head, and the other at the feet, where the body of Jesus had lain. And they say unto her, **Woman, why weepest thou?** She saith unto them, Because they have taken away my Lord, and I know not where they have laid him." John 20:12-13

The Special Meeting

Peter had been singled out from among the apostles for a special meeting with Jesus. There was something unsettled between Peter and Jesus. Peter had been feeling at his lowest these last three days. Peter had so miserably failed Jesus that night in the courtyards of Annas and Caiaphas. His denials of knowing Jesus still rang in the depth of his heart, and when Jesus had turned and looked at him, his heart melted within him. Tears blinding his eyes, he stumbled through the gate of the courtyard and out into the night beyond.

Somewhere that Sunday afternoon Jesus met with Peter. I would like to have been an unseen witness at that meeting. Can you imagine the surprise of Peter when Jesus appeared to him, and the joy of that moment when Peter realized that Jesus, who was crucified, was truly risen from the dead?

The details and the exact place of this meeting are shadowed in mystery. Here in this meeting Peter is forgiven and the joy of his relationship with Jesus is strengthened. The subject will not be brought up again. It was private between Peter and Jesus and needed no public exposure. Aren't you glad that your confession is between you and Jesus and requires no third party?

The Meeting is Twice Mentioned

This meeting of the resurrected Jesus and Peter is mentioned twice.

> "And they rose up the same hour, and returned to Jerusalem, and found the eleven gathered together, and them that were with them, Saying, The Lord is risen indeed, and hath appeared to **Simon**." Luke 24:33-34

Apparently Peter had already shared that at the group meeting in the upper room, the night after Easter Sunday. The group shared it with Cleopas and his wife, when they came back from Emmaus with another story of Jesus' appearance.

Paul, in his great treatise on the Resurrection in I Corinthians 15, cites a great number of witnesses of the Resurrection and among them he cites this appearance to Peter, giving no details other than the fact it happened.

> "And that he was buried, and that he rose again the third day according to the scriptures: And that he was seen of Cephas, then of the twelve:" I Corinthians 15:4-5

The Road North to Emmaus – The Fourth Recorded Appearance of Jesus

Place: Road to Emmaus Date: Sunday 17 Nisan AD 30

Time: Later Afternoon

It is late Sunday afternoon, the Sabbath travel restrictions have been lifted and Cleopas and his wife, Mary, were going home. They lived in the little village of Emmaus about seven miles northwest of Jerusalem. Some think that the person with Cleopas was another man, also a disciple of Jesus, but it seems more likely that it was his wife.

All the events of the week were flooding their souls; their beloved Jesus had been crucified. The horrible scene of Calvary was still fresh in their minds. The Hope of Israel was sleeping the sleep of death in the dark cavern of Joseph's tomb. Was the hope of the Messiah and Israel's redemption gone forever? Why had God allowed this to happen? Could not the God of all the universe turned the tide and save Jesus from the wicked high priests and from a mob controlled by their cohorts? Would all their dreams rest forever in a tomb in Jerusalem? God's plan of redemption was not yet clear in their thinking. Did they not know that Jesus must suffer and die for our salvation?

Their conversation about the events of the last week turned to the red-hot topic of this morning's report of an empty tomb. Mary had been deeply associated with the events of these last days. She had been one of the women who had stood near the cross during the hours of that horrible crucifixion. She had heard His words from the cross and had most likely been there when Jesus was taken from the cross and carried to Joseph's new tomb in the nearby garden. Like the other women, Mary had waited through the three days for the first of the week and had joined the group of ladies going to the tomb to complete final burial rites for Jesus.

This would be one of the most exciting and yet probably the most confused mornings of her entire life. It was apparent, even in the darkness, to see that the stone was rolled back from the door of the tomb. The open door surely meant that the tomb was empty. The Roman detachment of soldiers had disappeared sometime last night. The garden was empty, very quiet, and still bathed in the last shadows of night.

The women had come to the garden together for companionship, but mostly for mutual support. At the first sight of the moved stone and the exposed gaping hole into the tomb, Mary Magdalene went flying out of the garden toward Jerusalem to bring help.

As a group, the ladies first peered into the darkness of the tomb, and gaining courage, they entered. Two young men in white apparel greeted them. Sometime earlier in the night, one of these same angels had rolled away the stone and set on it, allowing the Roman soldiers to see him. He had thrown them into shock and then into panic.

Now inside the tomb, he is joined by another angel. They had a message from the Lord...

> "He is not here: for he is risen, as he said. Come, see the place where the Lord lay. And go quickly, and tell his disciples that he is risen from the dead; and, behold, he goeth before you into Galilee; there shall ye see him: lo, I have told you." Matthew 28:6-7

Angels, you say? At least that was what the women believed them to be. The Scripture is plain enough, it states clearly that they were angels; however, remember these young men in glowing white apparel had not introduced themselves to the women in any way. I do not believe there was a single doubt in the women's mind that these were indeed angelic beings, but there were those who were not sure of what the women had seen.

The group of women had separated as they left the tomb area. Mary had not been with the women on the road to Bethany that morning when Jesus appeared to them. She may have been en route to any one of the other destinations where the disciples had been staying. Therefore, Mary had missed seeing Jesus on that first Easter Sunday morning.

The exciting news of the women was soon to fall on ears that had been dulled by lack of faith. The apostles and disciples reckoned that what the women must have seen was a vision, perhaps one that they wanted to see and they gave it no credibility at all, simply calling it "visionary".

> "It was Mary Magdalene, and Joanna, and Mary the mother of James, and other women that were with them, which told these things unto the apostles. And their words seemed to them as idle tales, and they believed them not." Luke 24:10-11

That too might have been a disputable matter between the two of them. Mary would know what she had seen and heard, but would Cleopas believe her? Would not, he too think that it had only been a visionary; after all, five women in a dark tomb just might see a vision.

The Stranger from Galilee

The couple was so engrossed in their conversation that they were virtually unaware of other travelers on the road. Since travel had just opened after three days, there might have been many travelers coming and going. A gentleman joins with them in their discussion. Carefully, Jesus conceals His true identity, just as He had done after He had spoken in the service on that long ago Sabbath in His home synagogue in Nazareth. Deeply offended at Jesus' claim that Isaiah 61:1-2a were fulfilled in Him, they sought to cast Him over the hillside bluff to His death, but Jesus simply walked through the midst of them unrecognized and had escaped their rage.

Jesus asked them what they were talking about and why they were sad? Cleopas answered, "Are you a stranger in Jerusalem? Don't you know the things that have happened these last few days?" Jesus said, "What things?" And Cleopas launched into his story of the crucifixion and burial of Jesus. He didn't forget to mention that the women had reported an empty tomb and did not find Jesus' body and that certain of the apostles also went to the tomb and had reported the same. Cleopas did mention the women and the angels but allowed that the women had seen only a vision of angels with a visionary message.

Without revealing His true identity, Jesus said unto them...

> "O fools, and slow of heart to believe all that the prophets have spoken: Ought not Christ to have suffered these things, and to enter into his glory? And beginning at Moses and all the prophets, he expounded unto them in all the scriptures the things concerning himself." Luke 24:25b-27

How quickly the miles had flown away; they were even now arriving at the front door of their home in Emmaus. The Stranger made as though He would go on down the street, when suddenly their manners returned. "Come," they said, "have supper with us the day is late spend the night." The Stranger's company had been so exciting and in His explanation and comments the Scriptures became a Living Book to them.

It was time for the evening meal and they set down together. As a guest, the Stranger was asked to say the table grace. Picking up a loaf of bread, He blessed it and broke a piece for each. Suddenly their eyes were opened, it is Jesus! Together they had seen Him. Did Jesus just disappear? The word "vanished" is used. More than likely the meal was concluded and then Jesus disappeared from their sight as He left them. However, to disappear was not an improbability.

Wonderful truth, how sweet the sound! Jesus is alive and we have seen Him! We should have known that it was Jesus all along. Did not our hearts burn within us when He talked with us on the way and opened to us the Scriptures?

Darkness had fallen but they must return to Jerusalem tonight. Cleopas and Mary knew Peter had called a meeting of the apostles and a few disciples for tonight at Mary's house in Jerusalem. It had been kept quiet, for they were afraid of the situation in the city. The authorities were up in arms, afraid of a riot among the Galileans. News now of Jesus' resurrection had hit the streets of Jerusalem and it was far more powerful than the lie that the high priests had hired the Roman sentries to tell. There was a new fervor among the authorities to rid themselves of this troublesome group of Galileans.

Hastily, Cleopas and Mary's feet fell on the stones of the road back to Jerusalem. Would the apostles and disciples still be in the Upper Room? Hurry, Hurry, we must hurry, news like this cannot wait until tomorrow! Tomorrow some of them might be gone to Galilee or back to Perea. The message must be delivered tonight. Tired as they must have been, I can picture them at the fastest walk and often perhaps a short burst of speed.

They would have burst into Upper Room had the door not be locked, but it was. Rapid knocking brought someone to the door that recognized their voices. Soon the door was opened and they were inside. Someone blurted out, "The Lord is risen indeed, and hath appeared to Peter." And then Cleopas and Mary tells the story of meeting the Stranger on the road home and how they had recognized Him in their home.

Even while they were talking, Jesus Himself stood in the midst of them, and saith unto them...

> "Peace be unto you." Luke 24:36b

The Resurrection

Chapter Thirty-Nine

To the Ten Apostles – The Fifth Recorded Appearance of Jesus

Place: Jerusalem, the Upper Room Date: 18 Nisan AD 30

Time: Early Monday Night[1]

Apparently, Peter had called a secret meeting of the apostles on Easter Sunday night having met with Jesus earlier that afternoon. It would be important that they all know the wonderful truth of His Resurrection. It may be, although we do not know for sure, that Jesus asked Peter to call the meeting. We do not know everyone there; however, we do know who was missing among the apostles, Thomas and of course, Judas Iscariot, who was already dead by his own hand.

[1] The Jewish day begins with sundown. To us, this it would simply be Sunday night.

Why didn't Thomas attend the meeting? We do not know; however, we do know that he was very skeptically about the Resurrection reports, first of those by the women and perhaps later by Peter. His skepticism had alienated him from the group, so he did not join with them.

What do we really know about this Thomas? All three synoptic Gospels mention him in the list of the apostles.

> "Now the names of the twelve apostles are these; The first, Simon, who is called Peter, and Andrew his brother; James the son of Zebedee, and John his brother; Philip, and Bartholomew; **Thomas,** and Matthew the publican; James the son of Alphaeus, and Lebbaeus, whose surname was Thaddaeus; Simon the Canaanite, and Judas Iscariot, who also betrayed him." Matthew 10:2-4

> "And he ordained twelve, that they should be with him, and that he might send them forth to preach, And Simon he surnamed Peter; And James the son of Zebedee, and John the brother of James; and he surnamed them Boanerges, which is, The sons of thunder: And Andrew, and Philip, and Bartholomew, and Matthew, and **Thomas,** and James the son of Alphaeus, and Thaddaeus, and Simon the Canaanite, And Judas Iscariot, which also betrayed him: and they went into an house." Mark 3:14&16-19

> "And when it was day, he called unto him his disciples: and of them he chose twelve, whom also he named apostles; Simon, (whom he also named Peter,) and Andrew his brother, James and John, Philip and Bartholomew, Matthew and **Thomas**, James the son of Alphaeus, and Simon called Zelotes, And Judas the brother of James, and Judas Iscariot, which also was the traitor." Luke 6:13-16

Thomas had been with Jesus in Jerusalem in December when the Jews had sought His life. The whole group had retired across Jordan into Perea, where they spent the next three months. News came of the illness of Lazarus of Bethany and Jesus made plans to return to Bethany to see the family. Thomas knew the journey would be one of hazard, but he was utterly loyal to Jesus. Whether his statement, *"Let us also go, that we may die with him." John 11:16b* was one of irony or sincere commitment, it reflected the loyalty of a true follower. It is doubtful that his loyalty to Jesus could be questioned.

He said the following to Jesus after the sermon in John 14...

> "And whither I go ye know, and the way ye know. **Thomas saith unto him, Lord, we know not whither thou goest; and how can we know the way?"** John 14:4-5

We can thank Thomas for his question, for Jesus gave us a great verse in answering Thomas.

> "Jesus saith unto him, I am the way, the truth, and the life: no man cometh unto the Father, but by me." John 14:6

However, it is pretty apparent that Thomas is not a man that takes anything for granted. He was not convinced of the certainty of the Resurrection and he was not about to be in that meeting tonight.

John described the beginning of this meeting in the following way...

> "Then the same day at evening, being the first day of the week, when the doors were shut where the disciples were assembled for fear of the Jews, came Jesus and stood in the midst, and saith unto them, Peace be unto you." John 20:19

There certainly was reason for the apostles and disciples to fear the Jews, they were aware of the happenings of this day. They had heard the soldiers with their bribe money as they spread the lie about Jesus' body being stolen.

The high priests and temple authorities must have known about the reports being circulated among some of the Galileans. Some women had claimed that they had seen angels at the open tomb and some even claimed that they had seen Jesus. They certainly did not want "that rumor" to gain widespread acceptance. There was another question which must have troubled the high priest, "Why hadn't those Galileans gone home?" Where they waiting for Pentecost, which was fifty days away? Or were they just waiting for something to happen?

The Return of Cleopas and His Wife to Jerusalem

There was a knock on the door of the upper room, Cleopas and his wife had made the seven-mile trip back to Jerusalem to tell an exciting story. It unfolded in a matter of minutes, they were certain that He was indeed a risen Christ. Other testimonies were given, undoubtedly by the women and certainly by Peter. He may have withheld the details of the meeting, but he would never withhold the truth from the others.

Jesus Appears to all within the Room

Suddenly, Jesus was in the room greeting them with His familiar greeting, "*Shalom*" that is, "*Peace be unto you.*" At this meeting, John reports that He showed them His hands and side.

> "Then the same day at evening, being the first day of the week, when the doors were shut where the disciples were assembled for fear of the Jews, came Jesus and stood in the midst, and saith unto them, Peace be unto you. And when he had so said, he showed unto them his hands and his side. Then were the disciples glad, when they saw the Lord." John 20:19-20

Luke gives perhaps the clearest and strongest report of His appearance on that Sunday evening.

> "And as they thus spake, Jesus himself stood in the midst of them, and saith unto them, Peace be unto you. But they were terrified and affrighted, and supposed that they had seen a spirit. And he said unto them, Why are ye troubled? and why do thoughts arise in your hearts? Behold my hands and my feet, that it is I myself: handle me, and see; for a spirit hath not flesh and bones, as ye see me have. And when he had thus spoken, he showed them his hands and his feet. And while they yet believed not for joy, and wondered, he said unto them, Have ye here any meat? And they gave him a piece of a broiled fish, and of an honeycomb. And he took it, and did eat before them." Luke 24:36-43

This verse answers once and for all, the question, "Will the resurrected body have the ability to eat?" Did Jesus' body have that ability? Both Luke and John reported that He did eat before His disciples and with them.

Although Jesus had appeared behind closed doors, His body was of material substance. He was not just spirit, but in reality flesh and bone. When trying to explain this miracle, you might consider that He walked on the stormy waters of Galilee. He was, is, and will always be God with all His attributes and powers.

The Resurrection

Chapter Forty

Appearance to the Eleven – The Sixth Recorded Appearance of Jesus

Place: Jerusalem, the Upper Room | Date: 25 Nisan AD 30

Time: Early Monday [By our time, Sunday night]

It had been a long week for Thomas. All the rest of the apostles were filled with joy. They not only had seen Jesus, but they had seen and touched His hands and feet. There were great prints (scars) on His hands and feet where the nails had fastened Him to the cross only days ago. They were no longer the torn nail wounds, they were completely healed in His resurrected body. They are reminders of the price of our redemption, for all eternity they will remain the same. How do we know? The prophet Zechariah made us aware that the prints would still be there when he returned after the Tribulation for he wrote...

"And one shall say unto him, What are these wounds in thine hands? Then he shall answer, Those with which I was wounded in the house of my friends." Zechariah 13:6

Thomas had no such joy and he was as determined as ever that the whole group was entirely mistaken, for he said...

"But Thomas, one of the twelve, called Didymus, was not with them when Jesus came. The other disciples therefore said unto him, We have seen the Lord. But he said unto them, **Except I shall see in his hands the print of the nails, and put my finger into the print of the nails, and thrust my hand into his side, I will not believe.**" John 20:24-25

He absolutely could not be more positive than that. "I will not believe, unless I see in his hands the prints (scars) of the nails and put my finger into the nail holes and thrust my hand into His side." From this view Thomas got the title "the doubter"; however, the resurrection was incredible to Thomas. Yes, he had seen Jesus raise the dead, but that was a restoration to this life not something eternal. It just couldn't be true, he thought.

Had he only have been with them last Sunday night, he could have had the same information they had, the same assurance and with it the same joy. We miss so much because we miss Sunday night services. Don't you think that we could spare the Lord three or four hours on His day? It could change a doubter into a believer in just one evening.

Thomas Attends the Second Public Meeting

Another meeting had been called by the apostles in the upper room; there would be standing room only tonight. Although the meeting had been kept quiet, other believers would seek entrance to the building in hopes of seeing Jesus. What do you know? Thomas showed up, still looking for something spectacular. He remained non-committed from the beginning of the meeting. The meeting must have followed the lines of the old synagogues with Scripture reading, preaching, and periodic singing.

They did not begin gathering until the sun had slipped over the mountain and sank into the Mediterranean. Then they gathered only a few at a time and from different directions. Why? Because they did not want the meeting raided by the temple police and the apostles arrested.

A cool breeze blew eastward across the plains of Sharon as they gathered. One could not find a more peaceful setting or a more dangerous place to be if you were a follower of Jesus. The Jesus who had been crucified and was now reportedly risen from the dead. The disciples had shunned public gatherings during the day, fear still ran high among the group. They still remembered the power of the Jewish authorities and their political influence with the Romans.

The Holy Spirit will Come

None of them had the indwelling of the Holy Spirit nor the strength that would come from the indwelling presence of the Comforter. When He came, He would bring a boldness that would shock their enemies. He was the Paraclete, the one who came along side to be the believer's helper; however, He had not yet been given.

> "He that believeth on me *[Jesus]*, as the scripture hath said, out of his belly shall flow rivers of living water. (But this spake he of the Spirit, which they that believe on him should receive: for the Holy Ghost was not yet given; because that Jesus was not yet glorified.)" John 7:38-39

Jesus had made it clear that He would send a helper. He would be another Comforter, one just like Him. But the Comforter could not be sent prior to Jesus' becoming the believer's Mediator in heaven.

> "Nevertheless I tell you the truth; It is expedient for you that I go away: for if I go not away, the Comforter will not come unto you; but if I depart, I will send him unto you." John 16:7

The Upper Room

The upper room was blazing with stories and excitement. It was a meeting of discovery and joy. Some that had never saw the resurrected Christ were beginning to believe. They hung on every word of the testimony of those that had seen Him. After all, they were trustworthy witnesses and not some hysterical over-emotional mystics without common sense.

Thomas had brought his unbelief along to the meeting. He would not believe even after hearing every eyewitness account of the resurrection that was given that night. In fact, Thomas did not expect anything more to happen than what was happening already. I have known men like him. He probably was setting in the back, eaten up with grief, never for one moment allowing himself to believe. No! He must be satisfied with indisputable evidence.

Thomas was about to get the surprise of his life; suddenly Jesus was in the upper room. After His personal greeting to the group, the familiar, *"Peace be unto you,"* His eyes found Thomas and focused on him.

> "Then saith he *[Jesus]* to Thomas, Reach hither thy finger, and behold my hands; and reach hither thy hand, and thrust it into my side: and be not faithless, but believing." John 20:27

How did He know what Thomas had said about believing in the resurrection? Why did Thomas specify those very things? I believe Thomas probably uttered these words because the disciples had told him that Jesus had showed them His hands and His side and had invited them to handle Him. But there was his request for evidence, word for word just as he had spoken. What could Thomas say? What he did say was a great confession of faith?

> "And Thomas answered and said unto him, **My Lord and my God**." John 20:28

Did Thomas take Jesus' invitation and put his finger into the nail prints or thrust his hand into His side? I don't think so, but I do believe that he touched Him. The witnesses to the resurrection could not just see a form or figure, they had to touch and see that He was real, and on almost every occasion He gave them opportunity to do so.

The Resurrection

Chapter Forty-One

Jesus Surprises Seven Fishermen – The Seventh Recorded Appearance of Jesus

Place: At Peter's House in Capernaum | Time: A Few Days Later

The apostles had probably left Jerusalem after the second Sunday night meeting. A few days had passed and nothing more had happened to them. Other meetings may have been taking place, but they would know nothing of them.

Peter was not one to sit idle. He had to do something and fishing was in his blood. Were funds running low? Did Zebedee, James, and John's father need help with his fishing business or was it a little bit of rebellion in Peter. After all, Jesus had called him from the nets to become fishers of men.

The group meeting at Peter's house consisted of himself, Thomas, Nathanael (Bartholomew), James, John and two unnamed disciples.

Peter broke the monotony with three words, *"I go fishing."* The others quickly concurred, *"we also go with thee."*

Fishing by Night on the Sea of Galilee

They pushed out into the sea in their fishing vessels, familiar craft they were. They were rigged for catching fish. With full nets they might put the thought of the last few days behind them. They fished by night not far from the shoreline; here the fish came in at night to feed, for the lake was very deep.

It had been a wasted night; they had caught absolutely nothing. Now remember that these were experienced fishermen. Were they too troubled in their thoughts to do a good job fishing? Did they feel out of place? Who can know?

A small fire could be seen near the shoreline and in the dim light of morning, a figure could be seen walking along the shore near the water line. Who was this person? It was probably some early morning fisherman.

The figure was directly in the line of their fishing vessel when the man called out to them. It was the traditional question of every person who ever approached anyone fishing. *"Children, have ye any meat?"* And they gave the standard answer. *"No."* Jesus invited them to try the right side of the ship, apparently they had been fishing on the left. The nets were cast and they came up full.

Recognition

John said, "It is the Lord." Peter would not wait, but dived overboard swimming the three hundred or so feet to the shore. The others came, pulling the over laden net to land.

Now they could see that little fire clearly. It had bread and fish on it, but there was not enough for all, so Jesus called them to bring over part of their catch for the breakfast. Not one of them asked who He was, they knew Him immediately.

A Cozy Breakfast

What a pleasant morning it must have been, sitting around the fire, eating bread and fish, and watching the sun come up over the eastern hills of the lake. There had been no rebuke of their conduct nor had there been any approval.

Breakfast was ending, what would be next? Would Jesus just disappear or would their be a lesson or some specific instructions for the group? John, from the prospective of sixty-five years, remembered well the events of that morning.

Dost Thou Love Me?

When breakfast was over, Jesus turned to Peter and begin to ask him three personal but revealing questions. He gave him almost the same command following each answer. Some have erroneously taught that Jesus was giving Peter an opportunity to affirm his love for Jesus because he had denied Him three times at the enemy's fire in the high priest's courtyard. This was not true, that matter was settled on Easter Sunday afternoon when Jesus and Peter met. Because He is God, Jesus would never bring it up again. When your sins are forgive they are also forgotten.

> "And their sins and iniquities will I remember no more." Hebrews 10:17

Jesus Teaches the Only True Motivation for Service

> "So when they had dined, Jesus saith to Simon Peter, **Simon, son of Jonas, lovest thou me more than these?** He saith unto him, **Yea, Lord; thou knowest that I love thee**. He saith unto him, **Feed my lambs**." John 21:15

Peter do you *"agape"* me? The Greek word agape was a very strong word for love, a love like God gives. More than what? The fishing boat, the fish in the net, or the other disciples sitting around? More than what? Peter couldn't quite handle the strong Greek word so he replied, "Lord, thou knowest that I 'Philo' you." "Philo" is a weaker Greek word that means brotherly love. Accepting his answer, Jesus simply said, *"Feed my lambs."* These would be the baby or immature Christians that are often difficult to feed and require great effort. Here, Peter is given the motive of feeding lambs, loving me.

Again the question was asked. Jesus used the same Greek word of love and Peter again choosing the weaker word, answered Him. Again Jesus accepted his answer and said, *"Feed my sheep."* These are the more mature believers who are often stubborn and require much patience. Peter here is your motive for feeding the sheep, loving Jesus.

The question is asked a third time, but Jesus now uses the same Greek word as Peter, "Peter, do you 'philo' me?" A little upset at being asked three times, he replies...

> "He saith unto him the third time, Simon, son of Jonas, lovest thou me? Peter was grieved because he said unto him the third time, Lovest thou me? And he said unto him, **Lord, thou knowest all things; thou knowest that I love thee**. Jesus saith unto him, **Feed my sheep**." John 21:17

Peter sincerely used the same Greek word for love as he had previous used. Jesus accepted it and again said, *"Feed my sheep."* Peter here is your motive for feeding sheep, loving me.

But why three times? Because it is the law of teaching. Unless we get the motive for service right, we are a failure. Whatever you do, do it because you love the risen Christ.

Two Other Pieces of Information on the Seashore

Peter was told how he would die. We are not given the information how it would happen. But that day Peter knew, he did not know when and perhaps he did not know where, but he knew he would die a martyr's death.

Being human, Peter turned and asked about John. What would become of him? Jesus reminded Peter that it was his duty to follow Him and not to pay attention to how others were treated. The words of Jesus were plain and clear.

> "Then Peter, turning about, seeth the disciple whom Jesus loved following; which also leaned on his breast at supper, and said, Lord, which is he that betrayeth thee? Peter seeing him saith to Jesus, Lord, and what shall this man do? Jesus saith unto him, If I will that he tarry till I come, what is that to thee? follow thou me."[1] John 21:20-22

It had been rumored in the church that John would not die until Jesus returned. That was an error, a misinterpretation of what Jesus had actually said. John retells the events so the church will know the truth.

---

[1] The Church had built a false doctrine around this statement. For many were saying that John would live until the return of Christ. John points out in verse 23 that Jesus did not say that at all.

The Resurrection

Chapter Forty-Two

A Prescheduled Meeting – The Eighth Recorded Appearance of Jesus

Place: Galilee, at a Mountain Appointed but Unlisted Date: Zif AD 30

Matthew alone reports this meeting,[1] it was the first scheduled meeting announced. It was first announced at the garden tomb by the angels who told the women to carry the message to the apostles and disciples.

> "He is not here: for he is risen, as he said. Come, see the place where the Lord lay. And go quickly, and tell his disciples that he is risen from the dead; and, behold, he goeth before you into Galilee; there shall ye see him: lo, I have told you." Matthew 28:6-7

Jesus confirmed the meeting to the women on the road to Bethany, only a short time after His first appearance to Mary.

---

[1] This meeting seemed limited to only the eleven apostles and took place some days after the meeting with the fishermen at the Sea of Galilee.

> "And as they went to tell his disciples, behold, Jesus met them, saying, All hail. And they came and held him by the feet, and worshipped him. Then said Jesus unto them, Be not afraid: go tell my brethren that they go into Galilee, and there shall they see me." Matthew 28:9-10

In all the other meetings this scheduled meeting had not been forgotten. But before it happened, the fact of His resurrection would need to be clearly established. Once this had happened the meeting took place, right on Jesus' schedule.

The actual time and place of this meeting had been kept secret. It would be one of those private instructive commissioning meetings of Jesus and the apostles, numbering now only eleven. There would be no crowds gathering and no fanfare, but only the delivering of the great commission to be given to His Church.

The mountain must have been well known to the apostles. There were many historical mountains in the vicinity; however, I would opt for the mountain where the Beatitudes were given. It is a mountain that rises behind Capernaum and from its height, the beautiful blue Sea of Galilee shimmers in the sunlight and fields and villages spread out dotting the fertile countryside. What a place to give the great commission, for their world stretched before them, but it was about to be enlarged beyond their present comprehension.

The Great Commission

When they saw Him they all, without exception, worshipped Him, [2] but some doubted. What do you mean? Did they doubt His bodily resurrection? I think not, that had been established clearly in those two upper room meetings. None of them had been excluded; even Thomas who missed the first meeting was present at the second.

The word *doubt* used here is the Greek word *edistasan.* Its meaning is clearly seen not in the doubt of the reality of His resurrection, but in their doubt of their own ability and hesitation at their responsibility to preach the Gospel to all nations. Soon, and they knew it all too well now, Jesus would be on His way to Heaven. Hadn't He said that several times in His sermon in the upper room on the night of His betrayal? When He was arrested and taken away, they acted like cowards fleeing into the night and scattering like sheep on the hills of Judea.

What would they do now in those crisis situations that were bound to come in the preaching of the Gospel? There was so much to overcome, so much to learn, so much shyness to lose, and so much boldness to gain. Jesus took away some of their doubts with the assurance of both His ability and His power.

> "And Jesus came and spake unto them, saying, **All power is given unto me in heaven and in earth."** Matthew 28:18

---

[2] Worship means to recognize that He was God the Son and worthy of all glory, honor, and praise.

Only moments later, He would give them all the assurance they needed.

> "and, lo, I am with you alway, even unto the end of the world. Amen." Matthew 28:20b

These men would be the instruments to start and instruct the Church. The doctrine of the Church would wear their title for years to come, *The Apostles Doctrine.* You have a copy of that doctrine book; it is called the New Testament. The Holy Spirit produced it through these men. It is not their opinions, but the very Words of God Himself. They would have all the power they needed in just a few days; Jesus would remind them again as He had in John's Gospel of just how that would happen.

The Divine Commission Given

The great commission breaks down into three parts, and none are to be omitted. There is an absolute divine order given in the three parts, each must follow in its proper order. The first part of the commission is **evangelization, the making of disciples.** After a disciple is made he or she must be brought into the local fellowship of believers, which is the Church, and so we have **believer's baptism, signaling a union with Christ and His Church.** We are ready now, and only now, for the final part of the great commission, **"teaching them to observe all things which I have commanded you."** The teaching of all things continues for a lifetime, but has and holds its beginning in the fellowship of the believers and the Church.

> "Then the eleven disciples went away into Galilee, into a mountain where Jesus had appointed them. And when they saw him, they worshipped him: but some doubted. And Jesus came and spake unto them, saying, All power is given unto me in heaven and in earth. Go ye therefore, and teach all nations, baptizing them in the name of the Father, and of the Son, and of the Holy Ghost: Teaching them to observe all things whatsoever I have commanded you: and, lo, I am with you alway, even unto the end of the world. Amen." Matthew 28:16-20

Perhaps at this meeting, a larger meeting was called in which the apostles would share this information and Jesus would meet with a large group of the disciples. We cannot believe the next meeting was by chance, for Jesus is a God of order, plan, and purpose.

Chapter Forty-Three

The Largest Group Appearance of Jesus – The Ninth Recorded Appearance of Jesus

Place: Galilee, an Undisclosed Mountain

Date: Late Zif or Early Sivan AD 30 Time: Early Morning

What mountain? Was it still the mountain where the Sermon on the Mount was delivered, which was called the Mount of Beatitudes? Or was it that spectacular mountain where Peter, James, and John had witnessed the transfiguration of Jesus before their very eyes and had seen and heard Jesus talking with Moses and Elijah about the coming events at Jerusalem? This would forever be a sacred mountain to Peter. He remembered the events here as the greatest of his experiences, even as he faced death thirty-seven years later.

> "Knowing that shortly I must put off this my tabernacle, even as our Lord Jesus Christ hath showed me. Moreover I will endeavour that ye may be able after my decease to have these things always

> in remembrance. For we have not followed cunningly devised fables, when we made known unto you the power and coming of our Lord Jesus Christ, but were eyewitnesses of his majesty. For he received from God the Father honour and glory, when there came such a voice to him from the excellent glory, This is my beloved Son, in whom I am well pleased. And this voice which came from heaven we heard, when we were with him in the holy mount. We have also a more sure word of prophecy; whereunto ye do well that ye take heed, as unto a light that shineth in a dark place, until the day dawn, and the day star arise in your hearts: Knowing this first, that no prophecy of the scripture is of any private interpretation. For the prophecy came not in old time by the will of man: but holy men of God spake as they were moved by the Holy Ghost." II Peter 1:14-21

This would have been an ideal mountain since it was probably somewhere secluded and was possibly large enough to accommodate the crowd. However, the location of the mountain is of little significance. The fact that the meeting occurred is the valuable piece of information that we need.

Paul alone tells of this great meeting. The meeting was made known to him either through the revelation of Jesus as He taught him those three years in Arabia or perhaps the apostles shared this meeting with Paul at some other meeting that they had.

> "Neither went I up to Jerusalem to them which were apostles before me; but I went into Arabia, and returned again unto Damascus. Then after three years I went up to Jerusalem to see Peter, and abode with him fifteen days." Galatians 1:17-18

Paul was in a tough situation down at Corinth. The church had Jews but it was largely Greek and even the Jews had been dominated by Greek influence. Greeks had no problem believing in God. They had gods aplenty; superstition reigned in their religious thoughts and philosophy. They had no problem with the immortality of the soul; however, they did not believe it was even possible for the body to experience a resurrection.

To the Greeks the body was inherently evil with no possibility of redemption. This had permeated the church and they were denying the bodily resurrection of Jesus. The bodily resurrection of Jesus is not an option in Christian religion; it is an absolute truth. Paul would devote the full fifty-eight verses of I Corinthians 15 to the doctrine of the bodily resurrection. Paul spelled it out quite clearly...

> "For I delivered unto you first of all that which I also received, how that Christ died for our sins according to the scriptures; And that he was buried, and that he rose again the third day according to the scriptures:" I Corinthians 15:3-4

> "But if there be no resurrection of the dead, then is Christ not risen: And if Christ be not risen, then is our preaching vain, and your faith is also vain. Yea, and we are found false witnesses of God; because we have testified of God that he raised up Christ: whom he raised not up, if so be that the dead rise not. For if the dead rise not, then is not Christ raised: And if Christ be not raised, your faith is vain; ye are yet in your sins. Then they also which are fallen asleep in Christ are perished. If in this life only we have hope in Christ, we are of all men most miserable." I Corinthians 15:13-19

Paul presents a great treatise on the resurrection, making comparison after comparison to assure them that in the resurrection human flesh remained human flesh and not something else.

To prove his point, Paul brought a host of reliable witnesses before them. First, the Scriptures, then Cephas (Greek for Peter), then the apostles (only eleven at this time, but stilled called The Twelve), then this great crowd who had all saw or touched Jesus or had some other type of evidence of a resurrected body. Then there was James, Jesus' half-brother, whom they would also know, then the apostles again, possibly at the ascension, and finally by Paul himself. Am I a liar? Have I borne false witness? If He had not risen, then Paul had indeed lied, but Jesus was alive. Paul said...

> "But now is Christ risen from the dead, and become the firstfruits of them that slept. For since by man came death, by man came also the resurrection of the dead. For as in Adam all die, even so in Christ shall all be made alive." I Corinthians 15:20-22

Paul, reporting this event some twenty-two years after it happened, told the Corinthians that although some of these five hundred witnesses had fallen asleep, the greater part of them were still alive. What a meeting this must have been. When those who had only heard about the resurrection now themselves became eyewitnesses of the greatest event in history. Jesus is alive! The grave is robbed of its victim by a triumphant Christ.

The Resurrection

Chapter Forty-Four

An Appearance Back Home in Nazareth – The Tenth Recorded Appearance of Jesus

Place: Galilee, Probably the Village of Nazareth[1] Date: Sivan AD 30

Neither the writers of the Gospels or Paul were attempting to list every single appearance of Jesus nor every individual to whom He appeared. They probably listed those who were the better known among them so as to give a viable witness to the resurrection. All the authors will give a significant number of appearances, far more than enough to establish the credibility of the resurrection.

"After that, he was seen of James;" I Corinthians 15:7a

In just seven words, Paul covered this resurrection appearance. It is mentioned nowhere else in the New Testament of Jesus making any resurrection appearance to His earthly family. But these seven words open a world of thought and speculation.

That Jesus cared deeply about His mother [2] became very apparent at the cross. In intense pain and agony, Jesus was nearing death, but He did not want His mother subjected to it any more. She was standing nearby, with John, the only apostle that was near the cross. Jesus was moved with great compassion.

> "When Jesus therefore saw his mother, and the disciple standing by, whom he loved, he saith unto his mother, Woman, behold thy son! Then saith he to the disciple, Behold thy mother! And from that hour that disciple took her unto his own home." John 19:26-27

Jesus had spent years in the carpenter shop making a living for His mother, four brothers, and His sisters. They were children of Joseph and Mary, but it was true that they refused to believe Him to be the Messiah. When we live with greatness, our eyes are often blinded by what we refuse to see.

> "Now the Jews' feast of tabernacles was at hand. His brethren therefore said unto him, Depart hence, and go into Judaea, that thy disciples also may see the works that thou doest. For there is no man that doeth any thing in secret, and he himself seeketh to

---

[1] This was where Jesus grew up and where he had spent most of the thirty years of His life. The place of the home and family He had left behind.

[2] Mary was the mother of the human nature of Jesus and a very important part of His early life and human development. It is tragic how the Catholic Church has dishonored her by trying to make her deity. Jesus was her Saviour just as He is ours. However, we must not dishonor Mary by failing to acknowledge that God had pronounced her blessed among women. For she had been singled out to become an instrument in the hands of God to bring the Saviour into the world.

> be known openly. If thou do these things, show thyself to the world. **For neither did his brethren believe in him**." John 7:2-5

Who were His brothers? Some try desperately to make Mary a perpetual virgin, which according to Matthew 1:25 she was not. For after the birth of Jesus, the relationship between Joseph and Mary was that of a normal husband and wife. There is no need for that nonsense, the family is listed.

> "And when the sabbath day was come, he [Jesus] began to teach in the synagogue: and many hearing him were astonished, saying, From whence hath this man these things? and what wisdom is this which is given unto him, that even such mighty works are wrought by his hands? Is not this the carpenter, **the son of Mary, the brother of James, and Joses, and of Juda, and Simon? and are not his sisters here with us?** And they were offended at him. But Jesus said unto them, A prophet is not without honour, but in his own country, and among his own kin, and in his own house." Mark 6:2-4

There should be no doubt in our mind or in our hearts that Jesus made an appearance to them. At least James and Jude became believers and later great preachers. Did the others now believe? I think they did. This meeting would have been very private and the most likely place for it to occur was in their home back in Nazareth.

If Jesus appeared to all, why is only James mentioned? We can only speculate on the appearance to the entire family, but that He met with James was clearly reported. James became the pastor of the great Jerusalem church, as the apostles under persecution fled to the countryside and begin their great work of evangelism. James is called, along with Peter and John, a pillar in the church.

"And when James, Cephas, and John, who seemed to be pillars, perceived the grace that was given unto me, they gave to me and Barnabas the right hands of fellowship; that we should go unto the heathen, and they unto the circumcision." Galatians 2:9

James - Pastor and Author

James is called an apostle; however, he was not one of the twelve. Perhaps it was as that of Barnabas, a title signifying their importance. James was the author of the first book of the New Testament, the book of James. He would certainly have been well known and so would his brother Jude, who became a preacher and perhaps an evangelist and preached as far away as Corinth. Jude also wrote a New Testament book nearly forty years after the resurrection.

What did Jesus say at this meeting? I can only imagine that it was similar to all the other resurrection appearances. James, now as a true believer in Jesus, becomes a reliable witness of His glorious resurrection. In my opinion, the entire family had seen and touched the risen Jesus.

The Resurrection

Chapter Forty-Five

The Last Appearance to the Apostles - The Eleventh Recorded Appearance of Jesus

Place: Mount of Olives[1] Date: Ten days before Pentecost - Tammuz

Apparently Jesus had called this meeting. It came forty days after Passover and ten days before Pentecost. Jesus had some final instructions and reminders to give the group, and He would bid them farewell from the Mount of Olives. On the Mount of Olives one can look over the wall into the temple itself. It was on this very road that Jesus had said the following...

> "O Jerusalem, Jerusalem, thou that killest the prophets, and stonest them which are sent unto thee, how often would I have gathered thy children together, even as a hen gathereth her chickens under her wings, and ye would not! Behold, your house is left unto you desolate." Matthew 23:37-38

[1] The Mount of Olives is located across the Kidron Valley from Jerusalem and in sight of Bethany.

After the greeting, Jesus opened their minds, that they might understand the Scriptures. Jesus said that they were to tarry at Jerusalem until they were endued [2] with power from on high. This is the coming of the Holy Spirit.

> "And said unto them, Thus it is written, and thus it behoved Christ to suffer, and to rise from the dead the third day: And that repentance and remission of sins should be preached in his name among all nations, beginning at Jerusalem. And ye are witnesses of these things. And, behold, I send the promise of my Father upon you: but tarry ye in the city of Jerusalem, until ye be endued with power from on high." Luke 24:46-49

Jesus had promised the coming of the Holy Spirit in John, telling the disciples that it was expedient that He go away. Jesus had to enter into the intercessory work before the Holy Spirit could be given.

> "And I will pray the Father, and he shall give you another Comforter,[3] that he may abide with you for ever; Even the Spirit of truth; whom the world cannot receive, because it seeth him not, neither knoweth him: but ye know him; for he dwelleth with you, and shall be in you." John 14:16-17

First Jesus tells them to tarry (wait without doing anything), and then Jesus gives them both the work and the program for evangelizing the world.

---

[2] Endued literally means to be clothed upon. They were to wait for the coming of the Holy Spirit.

[3] The word *Comforter* means to make strong. It is the Greek word Paraclete, which means one who comes along side of to help. The Holy Spirit not only dwells in us, He is our constant companion and helper.

> "But ye shall receive power, after that the Holy Ghost is come upon you: and ye shall be witnesses unto me both **in Jerusalem**, and in **all Judaea,** and in **Samaria**, and unto the uttermost part of the earth." Acts 1:8

Watching Until His Disappearance

The charge has been given and now it is time for Jesus to begin His great intercessory work in our behalf. With hands lifted in blessing, Jesus slowly begins to rise. The disciples are so engrossed in His going up that they hardly notice two men (angels) in white apparel standing and gazing up with them.

Soon Jesus was just a speck in the sky, and finally the clouds completely hid Him from view. No apostle could have watched such a sight without mixed emotions. The demonstration of Jesus' power must have been very dramatic; however, they knew that this was their last glimpse of Him until they went to heaven or until He returned.

Long after Jesus had disappeared, they stood gazing into the sky hoping for one last glimpse of their beloved Christ. From nearby, the angels spoke to them.

> "Which also said, Ye men of Galilee, why stand ye gazing up into heaven? this same Jesus, which is taken up from you into heaven, shall so come in like manner as ye have seen him go into heaven." Acts 1:11

Some want to believe that somehow Jesus changed on the way up to heaven and He became Spirit as God the Father and God the

Holy Spirit are; however, the testimony of prophecy, the testimony of Angels, and the witness of Paul said that Jesus retained the resurrected body and when He returns it will be in that resurrected body. In fact, He will bear it for all eternity.

> "And I will pour upon the house of David, and upon the inhabitants of Jerusalem, the spirit of grace and of supplications: and they shall look **upon me whom they have pierced**, and they shall mourn for him, as one mourneth for his only son, and shall be in bitterness for him, as one that is in bitterness for his firstborn." Zechariah 12:10

> "And one shall say unto him, What are these wounds in thine hands? Then he shall answer, Those with which I was wounded in the house of my friends." Zechariah 13:6

> "Which also said, Ye men of Galilee, why stand ye gazing up into heaven? this same Jesus, which is taken up from you into heaven, shall so come in like manner as ye have seen him go into heaven." Acts 1:11

> "For there is one God, and one mediator between God and men, the man Christ Jesus;" I Timothy 2:5

The Final Appearance – The Twelfth Appearance of Jesus

Place: Somewhere in Arabia [4] Date: About AD 37

> "And last of all he was seen of me also, as of one born out of due time. " I Corinthians 15:8

[4] This is the location in Arabia where Paul has spent three years with Jesus in training and receiving His revelations.

Paul calls this an appearance to one born of due time or season. In fact, this appearance came at least seven years after the others and after Jesus' ascension into heaven. There are those who believe that Paul became an eyewitness of the resurrection of Jesus on the Damascus road. True, he was struck down on the road by blinding light before he reached Damascus and in his blinded state acknowledged Jesus as Lord, but he had no way of telling if the body of Christ was real or just a vision or spirit. It would be in the desert of Arabia that Paul would get to know the reality of resurrection.

Paul - The Persecutor

> "For I am the least of the apostles, that am not meet to be called an apostle, because I persecuted the church of God." I Corinthians 15:9

There were many in Judea in the early 30's that did not believe in the resurrection of Jesus, and chief among them would have been Saul (Paul). He was a Pharisee, an officer of the Sanhedrin Court, and a zealous contender for their Jewish faith. He had been at the first martyrdom of this new faith. He had heard the moving sermon of this young man name Stephen and still he remained unconvinced.

This young fanatic, for that is what you call those who are ardent in their faith if it is different than your own, had sincerely believed in this new faith and had given his life for it. Maybe this created a little uncertainty in Saul's hard heart, but it did not win him over.

He was convinced that this new religious sect, yet unnamed excepted as followers of Jesus, was a serious threat to the religion he knew and followed from his youth. He was thoroughly convinced that he was serving God in trying to exterminate this new sect.

Today he was on the road to Damascus with arrest warrants in his pocket. He would arrest and bring the leaders of this new sect, soon to be called Christianity, to Jerusalem to face the Sanhedrin Court. Somewhere outside the city of Damascus Saul was overcome with a bright light and heard a voice from heaven saying...

> "And he fell to the earth, and heard a voice saying unto him, Saul, Saul, why persecutest thou me? And he said, Who art thou, Lord? And the Lord said, I am Jesus whom thou persecutest: it is hard for thee to kick against the pricks. And he trembling and astonished said, Lord, what wilt thou have me to do? And the Lord said unto him, Arise, and go into the city, and it shall be told thee what thou must do." Acts 9:4-6

Inside the city, Saul was led to a personal faith in Christ, probably by one of the men he came to arrest. Converted and baptized, Saul immediately began his ministry, preaching that Christ was the Son of God in the synagogues.

So elegant was his speech and so logical was his doctrine and presentation, that soon he was in trouble with the Jewish element in Damascus. They were able to set the governor on him. The brethren feared for his life and helped him escape by lowering him over the wall in a basket.

Away to Arabia

"But when it pleased God, who separated me from my mother's womb, and called me by his grace, To reveal his Son in me, that I might preach him among the heathen; immediately I conferred not with flesh and blood: **Neither went I up to Jerusalem to them which were apostles before me; but I went into Arabia, and returned again unto Damascus. Then after three years I went up to Jerusalem to see Peter,** and abode with him fifteen days." Galatians 1:15-18

Paul much needed the training that all the apostles received, so for the next three years he was alone in Arabia. Jesus must have made frequent appearances to Paul teaching and making revelations. Paul was the greatest theologian of the New Testament, bringing both the Old Testament and the New together in fulfillment.

In order to be an apostle, Paul must be personally called by Jesus Christ, be personally trained by Him, and finally he must be an eyewitness of the resurrection. Here in the lonely desert, this was all fulfilled. There was no doubt in this former persecutor; he was convinced that Jesus had bodily risen from the dead. He wrote the greatest statement of the bodily resurrection of Jesus and those who sleep in Him.

Even the unsaved will have a bodily resurrection and stand in the final judgment, not as a spirit but as human beings. After the judgment, body, soul, and spirit will be cast into the lake of fire.

Paul assured them that there would be no more resurrection appearances, he certainly had listed more than an adequate number in I Corinthians 15. Paul would be the last, there would be no more apostles, for Paul was the last chosen one. They would be responsible as witnesses of Jesus' resurrection to bear witness to that very fact. They were responsible for the doctrine of the New Testament, and every book in it is either written by an apostle or someone in close contact with the apostles. The New Testament is rightly called the Apostles' Doctrine.

Conclusion

I believe Luke when he said...

> "he [Jesus] showed himself alive after his passion by many infallible proofs," Acts 1:3b

And I fully believe his report from the upper room...

> "Jesus himself stood in the midst of them, and saith unto them, Peace be unto you. But they were terrified and affrighted, and supposed that they had seen a spirit. And he said unto them, Why are ye troubled? and why do thoughts arise in your hearts? **Behold my hands and my feet, that it is I myself: handle me, and see; for a spirit hath not flesh and bones, as ye see me have. And when he had thus spoken, he showed them his hands and his feet. And while they yet believed not for joy, and wondered, he said unto them, Have ye here any meat?** And they gave him a piece of a broiled fish, and of an honeycomb. And he took it, and did eat before them. And he said unto them, These are the words which I spake unto you, while I was yet with you, that all things must be fulfilled, which were written in the law of Moses, and in the prophets, and in the psalms, concerning me. Then opened he their understanding, that they might understand the scriptures," Luke 24:36b-45

He lives, forever He lives! Christ Jesus Lord of all, conqueror of death, and giver of eternal life to those who believe in Him!

Research References

Carr, Dr. Harry E. Just About... Angels. Kearney, NE: Morris Publishing Company, 2001.

Carr, Dr. Harry E. This I Believe. Kearney, NE: Morris Publishing Company, 1999.

Comay, Joan and Ronald Brownrigg. Who's Who in the Bible. New York, NY: Random House Publishing, 1952.

Davies, Benjamin, editor. Baker's Harmony of the Gospels. Grand Rapids, MI: Baker Book House, 1983.

Robertson, A.T. A Harmony of the Gospels. New York, NY: Harper & Brothers, 1950.

Shepard, J.W. The Christ of the Gospels. Grand Rapids, MI: Eerdmans Publishing Company, 1939.

Note: The material listed above was simply used as general reference material, no quotes were made, except from the author's own published works.